Greenberg's Guide to M.T.H. Electric Trains: First Edition

As you read the First Edition and compare the listings in the book with your own items, you may discover variations and/or additional information about the items reported in this book. We are interested in learning about these differences so we may include them in the Second Edition. Also, should you spot any errors, please let us know.

This is_____an addition,_____a correction,_____a variation.

Item number_____.

Category: Premier steam_____diesel_____passenger_____freight_____.
RailKing steam_____diesel_____passenger_____freight_____.
Tinplate Traditions _____.

Major body color:_____Minor body color _____

Body is _____painted_____unpainted.

Major lettering color _____Other lettering color_____.

Lettering is_____rubber-stamped_____heat-stamped.

Road name or herald_____.

Estimated production date _____Cataloged?_____Yes_____No.

Other information (please use additional paper if needed):

If you have a photograph of the subject, please include it with your report.
Thank you for your assistance.

Name:

Street:

City/State:

Phone:_____e-mail_____.

Please return to: Editor, M.T.H., Kalmbach Books, 21027 Crossroads Circle, Waukesha, WI 53187

If you have multiple listings, please make copies of this sheet and submit them as well.

If you're knowledgeable about current prices of MTH trains and would like to be considered as a price contributor, please check here_____.

GREENBERG'S®
GUIDE TO
M.T.H. Electric Trains®

KALMBACH
BOOKS

Printed in Canada

99 00 01 02 03 04 05 06 07 08   10 9 8 7 6 5 4 3 2 1

Visit our website at
http://books.kalmbach.com
Secure online ordering available

Publisher's Cataloging in Publication
(Provided by Quality Books, Inc.)

Greenberg's guide to MTH electric trains — 1st ed.
    p. cm.
    Includes index.
    ISBN: 0-89778-454-5

    1. Railroads—Models.

  TF197.G74 1999   625.1'9
                          QBI99-1210

Book and cover design: Kristi Ludwig

Contents

Foreword

Model railroading—an institution in the hobby industry and a tradition among families everywhere—has added a whole new dimension to my life over the years. The personal economic rewards of owning and operating M.T.H. Electric Trains are obviously satisfying, but the significance of the relationships and bonds of friendship I have built within this environment are priceless. After 25 years of working in the realm of model railroading, the one truism that best describes the hobby is how special model railroaders are. Almost without exception I can sincerely state that the folks I have been fortunate enough to work and "play" with in this wonderful hobby have been characteristically friendly, caring, and kind . . . just really good people who are passionate about model railroading.

Over the years the hobby has grown, but along with that growth, the expectations of our customers have also increased. Although MTH's efforts to meet all of these expectations represent a major challenge, I have not found any of them to be unreasonable. After all, who could deny customers the opportunity to enjoy improved quality, variety, detail, and operating features in their model railroading purchases? Besides, it is the challenge to meet customer demands that is the driving force for an aggressive company like M.T.H. Electric Trains. In truth, this force keeps MTH positioned to capture market share from those firms not responding to customer requirements. While MTH has benefited from listening and responding to our customers' wishes, the entire model railroading world has benefited as well. In fact, never before has the O gauge model railroading community so enjoyed the variety of choices that is now available to them.

In just six years, M.T.H. Electric Trains introduced over 120 different motive power units, 80 different types of freight and passenger rolling stock, and dozens of new accessories. Factor in the different colors, diverse roadname schemes, and operating configurations, and you will find that O gauge enthusiasts are offered a menu of nearly 2,000 choices!

In recent years, other manufacturers have been diligent in trying to meet the consumer demand for variety and value, but M.T.H. Electric Trains has been out in front offering hobbyists several innovative features. MTH was first to initiate factory-installed digital sound systems, diesel engine smoke units, die-cast articulated steam engines in both scale and semi-scale proportions, a track system with a built-in roadbed, the first 400-watt UL approved transformer (when others said it couldn't be done), digital sound and operating smoke in tinplate locomotives, modular chassis design for simple and easy locomotive servicing, and starter train sets with digital sound. This is quite a list of accomplishments!

Our success and innovation have been possible only because we "keep our ears to the ground" when it comes to what our customers want and need. We thoughtfully consider all requests for new products and improvements in existing inventory. Above all, we consistently strive to find better, more-efficient ways to produce our products, employing the latest technology.

We have not been, nor will we ever be, content to rest on our successes. At M.T.H. Electric Trains we are continuously exploring new ideas and experimenting with new products. There are many more great surprises in store for model railroading fans, and MTH is excited about presenting them to you. Finally, MTH is fully committed to continue building on the reputation so many of you have helped us establish.

Mike Wolf

Acknowledgments

Having been professionally involved in the toy train hobby now for a dozen years (first as editor of *Classic Toy Trains* and now as editor-in-chief of Kalmbach/Greenberg Books), I'm no longer surprised by the eager willingness of toy train enthusiasts to pitch in and help out on a project. In the case of this book, the first edition of *Greenberg's Guide to M.T.H. Electric Trains,* the cooperation of numerous people has gone way beyond any expectations I could have had. Many, many thank-you's are due, so here goes:

To **Mike Wolf** for his genius in founding and guiding M.T.H. Electric Trains, and for providing the company's computer data base to us as the basis for the product listings. Also, thank you for opening your archives to us during the photo shoot.

To **Andy Edleman** from MTH for answering questions, providing lists, sending catalogs, and making his knowledge of MTH available to us.

To **Se Yong Lee** of Samhongsa for producing great trains and for taking the time to tell us about his company and his relationship with MTH.

To **Wilton Lash,** MTH collector, for absolutely unbelievable assistance by opening box after box of MTH trains for us to photograph and verify color and numbers.

To **Duke Lash** and to the **CWI crew** who helped unpack, transport, and repack all those trains—on a weekend, no less!

To **Jack Sommerfeld,** owner of Sommerfeld's Hobby Shop in Butler, Wisconsin, for spending the evening with us as we photographed his Standard gauge collection and for allowing Kent and me to get in the way of his customers as we recorded car numbers and colors from his inventory.

To **Steve Serenska,** president of BangZoom Software and producer of the TrainTracker inventory system, for crunching data and numbers to make the details as complete and accurate as possible.

To **Jack Schmidt** from MTH for ferrying trains back and forth for us and for bringing in trains from his own collection to help us make the book more complete.

To **Kris Kozub** for sharing his collection with us and to **Bob Keller** for hauling in his own predominately black-and-white trains so we could photograph them in color.

To **Bruce Greenberg** and all of the **Greenberg employees and authors** who long ago prepared the way for this book.

To **Bill Zuback** and **Jim Forbes** for spending long hours on the road photographing MTH cars and locomotives.

To **Kristi Ludwig** for creating a different and attractive design for the book and then completing the layout on time, even though we gave the book to you piecemeal.

To **Mary Algozin** for proofreading over and over all of the copy and for catching the errors.

And especially to **Kent Johnson,** acquisitions editor, for doing all the really hard work.

Finally, thank you to the **MTH fans** who provided price information, and to those we know will send us additional information so that the second edition will be better than the first!

I'm sure I've inadvertently left out some people. Please forgive me if I have. Let me know, and I'll correct that error in the next edition.

Dick Christianson
Editor-in-Chief
Kalmbach Books

How This Book Is Organized

WHAT PRODUCTS ARE LISTED
Inclusions and Exclusions

Greenberg's Guide to M.T.H. Electric Trains lists the full array of train and toy products that appeared in MTH's principal annual consumer catalogs between 1993 and 1999.

The following pages reflect a comprehensive list of products that was originally provided and verified by representatives of M.T.H. Electric Trains. Some items, however, were not available for viewing, and their descriptions were taken from MTH catalogs. Additionally, this first edition does not attempt to address uncataloged factory production or factory errors that may need further identification. In these cases, where details are missing or doubtful, we ask our readers for information.

HOW PRODUCTS ARE LISTED
Sections and Chapters

We have initially organized the contents according to their product line—Premier, RailKing, or Tinplate Traditions. Each section includes separate chapters of products classified as steam locomotives, diesel locomotives (including electric, turbine, and motorized units), rolling stock, or passenger cars. Accessories are listed in a simplified index format in an appendix at the back of the book.

Each chapter opens with an introduction that surveys all types of locomotives or cars in the category covered by that chapter. Unlike other toy train manufacturers, the number printed directly on MTH products does not reflect the number M.T.H. Electric Trains uses to catalog or inventory their production. Therefore, within these chapters you will find that we have further organized the products by specific and recognizable equipment type, relative size, and then product number. With the exception of steam locomotives, the types are listed in alphabetical order; the relative size (based on other products of the same type) is listed from smallest to largest; and the product numbers are listed in ascending numerical order.

The steam locomotives in this book are listed according to the well-established Whyte classification system. In this system, numerals represent the number of wheels in each group, starting at the front end of a locomotive: lead truck, drivers, trailing truck. Most wheel arrangements have names derived from the first users of the wheel arrangement. The list on the opposite page identifies the type and name of the wheel arrangements found in this book.

Line Listings

Each detailed listing includes a variety of descriptive elements. The manufacturer-assigned catalog number is the first identifying marker. The prefix of this number distinguishes between the various MTH product lines (e.g., 10-numbers designate the Tinplate Traditions line, 20-numbers designate the Premier line, 30-numbers designate the RailKing line, etc.). Items indicated by an asterisk immediately following the last digit of the catalog number were reviewed in the pages of *Classic Toy Trains* magazine.

The text description for most items identifies the road (railroad) name, equipment type, equipment number, primary and secondary colors, lettering, and year the item was first cataloged. When appropriate, other detailed data such as car loads, set contents, and product review references are also indicated in this description.

Buying and Selling Trains

First, consider the relative knowledge of the seller and buyer. A seller may not be aware that he has an exceptional item and sell it for the price of a common piece. Another source of price variation is short-term fluctuation, which depends on what is being offered at a given train meet on a given day. A related source of variation is the season of the year. Traditional train markets are less frequented in the summer, so sellers may at this time be more inclined to reduce prices. Another important source of price variation is the relative strength of the seller's desire to sell and the buyer's eagerness to buy. A final source of variation is the personalities of the seller and buyer.

We receive many inquiries as to whether or not a particular piece is a "good value." This book will help guide you to the answer, but there is no substitute for experience in the marketplace. We strongly recommend that novices do not make major transactions

Whyte Classification System

Type	Name	Wheel Arrangement
0-4-0	Four-Wheel Switcher	OO
0-8-0	Eight-Wheel Switcher	OOOO
2-4-2	Columbia	oOOo
2-6-0	Mogul	oOOO
2-8-0	Consolidation	oOOOO
2-8-4	Berkshire	oOOOOoo
2-6-6-6	Allegheny	oOOO OOOooo
2-8-8-2	Mallet Consolidation	oOOOO OOOOo
4-4-0	American, Eight-Wheeler	ooOO
4-4-2	Atlantic	ooOOo
4-4-4	Jubilee	ooOOoo
4-6-0	Ten-Wheeler	ooOOO
4-8-2	Mountain	ooOOOOo
4-8-4	Northern	ooOOOOoo
4-6-6-4	Challenger	ooOOO OOoo
4-8-8-2	Articulated Consolidation (Cab-Forward)	ooOOOO OOOOo
4-8-8-4	Big Boy	ooOOOO OOOOoo

without the assistance of friends who have experience in buying and selling trains.

Determining Values

In addition to offering an extensive list of products, we have also suggested fair market values for most items when there have been a sufficient number of reported sales. For these items, we provide two pricing categories: *Manufacturer's Suggested Retail Price (MSRP)* and *Current*.

The *MSRP* reflects the price established by the manufacturer at the time the item was first issued. Be aware that in some cases the manufacturer has amended the MSRP for subsequent releases of the same product.

We have indicated *Current* prices in this edition because of the significant portion of items offered at Like New (showing only the faintest signs of handling and wear) or better condition. The values in this category are based on obtained prices, rather than asking prices. Generally the prices reported here represent a "ready sale," or the price most likely to effect a quick sale.

We have indicated *CP* (Current Production) in the value column of some items. These items are now being advertised or manufactured, or they are readily available for purchase from current dealer stock at or near the MSRP.

Items that were cataloged or otherwise advertised, but never produced by the manufacturer, are designated with *NM* (Not Manufactured) in the value column. In a few instances, an *N/A* (Not Available) designation indicates that inadequate information was available at the time of publication.

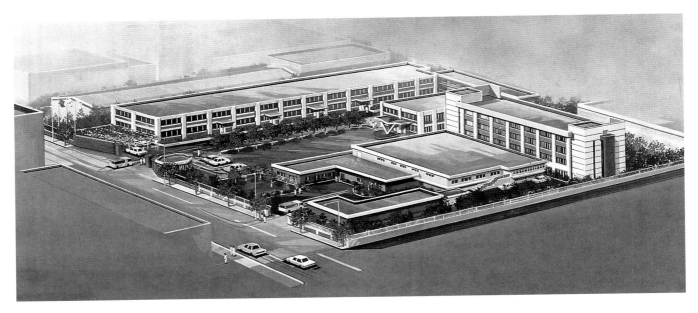

An artist's rendering of the Samhongsa factory in Seoul, South Korea.

Samhongsa
Where M.T.H. Electric Trains Come From

By Jim Caccavo

The M in MTH stands for Mike—Mike Wolf—the founder and owner of M.T.H. Electric Trains. Though less than a decade old, MTH is without question the fastest-growing O gauge three-rail electric train company in America today, and Mike

Mike Wolf, founder and owner of MTH Electric Trains, and Se Yong Lee, president and CEO of Samhongsa.

Wolf deserves a tremendous amount of credit for that success. From his youthful association with Williams Electric Trains, through his cooperative ventures with Lionel Trains Inc., to the development of his own enormously successful toy train business, Mike Wolf has become *the* force to be reckoned with in the three-rail O gauge industry.

However, Mike would be the first to admit that he has not created M.T.H. Electric Trains by himself. Among those he would acknowledge are family, friends, employees, suppliers, and other business partners. But perhaps highest on his list of friends is his South Korean manufacturing partner: Samhongsa.

The name "Samhongsa" was well known and respected in the scale model railroading hobby before most three-rail toy trains started arriving here from Asia. It is a name synonymous with quality in craftsmanship and product performance, and is acknowledged as being, in large part, responsible for the success of several model train companies worldwide, from N scale to No. 1.

MTH and Samhongsa have developed a strong working relationship, based on mutual respect and shared objectives—so much so that Samhongsa is now the exclusive manufacturer in O gauge for MTH, declining all O gauge, three-rail requests from other importers. In fact, this relationship has proved so successful that MTH is giving Lionel Trains its first serious competition since the first half of the 20th century.

IN THE BEGINNING

Samhongsa was founded in 1970 by Mr. Sang Man Lee. Today, 54-year-old Se Yong Lee, the son of Sang Man Lee, is president and CEO of the company.

For many years after the devastating Korean conflict of 1950–53, the Korean people struggled to survive and rebuild their nation. The 1970s brought continuing financial challenges to Korea and its people, and Sang Man Lee was forced to close the bookstore that provided his livelihood and find a new business by which he could support his family. A relative working in Japan suggested the brass model industry, since there was no competition in Korea at the time. Thus, when Japanese manufacturer Olympia sold them HO scale passenger car parts (for a Gem Imports model) to assemble as a subcontractor, Samhongsa became the first Korean brass modelmaker.

The company had humble beginnings. At first, it worked out of small quarters near the old South Gate Market in Seoul. Sang Man Lee and Se Yong Lee's uncle, Byung Sung Min (who later became Chairman of the Board for Samhongsa) began hiring temporary and part-time workers as needed. Shortly thereafter, Samhongsa, still working as a subcontractor, assembled its first locomotive, Gem's HO scale Pennsylvania RR N1s 2-10-2. This was followed by its first locomotive as prime contractor—an HO scale Baltimore & Ohio Dockside locomotive for Gem.

Those early years were hit and miss. Korea was industrially and politically unstable, and the economy was struggling. During those years, Se Yong Lee recalls, it was hard for his father to find subcontractors to make specific parts, and there was no machinery for any kind of miniature production.

CHALLENGES AND OPPORTUNITIES

After serving three years in the Korean Army, with one year in Vietnam, Se Yong Lee returned to civilian life and completed his college education. In 1973, at the age of 27, he joined his father's firm.

The company was having difficulty developing the market for model trains. By his own account, Se Yong Lee's father and uncle knew little about model trains. The orders from Gem were not large enough to sustain the company, and there were numerous complaints from customers. Though the Korean models were less expensive than the Japanese products, they were below the standard set by Japanese model trains. Nevertheless, even in those

An engineer compares a Budd RDC test shot against the CAD drawing of the model.

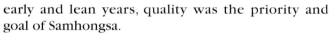
An employee applies lettering to a Santa Fe Budd RDC.

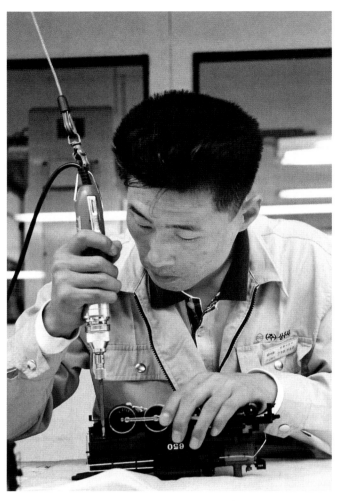
Power tools make assembly of the Camelback more efficient.

early and lean years, quality was the priority and goal of Samhongsa.

When Van Hobbies in Vancouver, Canada, started placing orders for Canadian-prototype models, things began to improve. Through that contact Samhongsa became acquainted with Pacific Fast Mail (PFM), which Van represented in Canada. In those days PFM was North America's major brass model importer and carried a portion of Van's Canadian production for sale in America. This was followed later with direct orders from PFM and, subsequently, Samhongsa's entry into the European market.

Samhongsa was on the track to success. The client list would grow to include Hallmark, Key, Sunset, Westside, Oriental, W&R, Precision Scale, Beaver Creek, Garden Railway Supply, Weaver, and Märklin.

SAMHONGSA AND MIKE'S TRAIN HOUSE

In 1985 Samhongsa broadened its horizons and began manufacturing micro motors, now used in

Canon cameras, CD-ROM drives, and other electronic devices. In the same year Se Yong Lee met an ambitious young American named Mike Wolf. Lee recalls 25-year-old Wolf coming to him with a tinplate cattle car reproduction project. Se Yong Lee's intention was to meet with Jerry Williams of Williams Electric Trains, but as Lee recalls, "He [Willams] was not interested and introduced Mike Wolf instead. From early on I was impressed with Mike's attitude and sincerity."

The Lionel Classic series for collectors was done by Samhongsa through Mike Wolf when Wolf was working with Lionel—Samhongsa never had a direct link with Lionel. The die-cast locomotives were to be the beginning of a new direction for Samhongsa, departing from the more-complicated and time-consuming all-brass models.

Samhongsa had prepared production lines for a Lionel O scale-sized Dash 8 locomotive for Lionel when the project fell through.

Partially assembled Camelbacks roll along the assembly line.

As Wolf recalled in a May 1998 *Classic Toy Trains* magazine interview, "They [Samhongsa] had a lot of people and overhead they had to continue to support, and I had an obligation to them to continue to support."

Wolf went ahead and announced the production of the scale-sized diesel locomotive, after which Lionel canceled the dealership status of his retail operations, leaving him with $750,000 worth of deposited orders that Lionel would not fulfill. Litigation that dragged on for three years finally got Mike Wolf paid.

But by now MTH and Samhongsa were rolling full steam. Wolf's respect for and consideration towards his Asian supplier would be remembered and returned tenfold in quality and craftsmanship. "I would not want to jeopardize my special relationship with Mike Wolf," reflected Se Yong Lee. "So I cannot produce O gauge for someone else who would in turn compete with Mike's Train House because I also consider him to be a good friend."

INSIDE SAMHONGSA

Inside the 27,329-square-foot plant in Seoul—where MTH products are assembled and painted—it's all business. You won't hear radios playing, and there is no talking or joking between the many young women (mostly) employees assembling MTH locomotives and cars. Instead, they work with absolute concentration on each and every product passing through their white-cotton-gloved hands, looking for the slightest flaw that will send the locomotive or car back to be corrected.

Mr. Ki Ho Sung, Director of the Model Train Division, explained that the first three locomotives of each product line are put through a grueling 100-hour test run before subsequent models are tested and packaged for shipping. Color schemes are checked against the actual prototype samples in a special room with daylight-balanced light to assure accuracy of the Union Pacific chrome yellow or the South Pacific Daylight orange.

THE BEGINNING OF A MODEL TRAIN

Every train product manufactured at Samhongsa starts with the customer coming to the company with drawings and photographs of the prototype. Careful staff evaluation of the project results in a bid to the client. Once the bid is accepted, the manufacturing process begins.

Samhongsa's designers and engineers make their own drawings from the prototype. With everything computerized now, drawings of each part can be done more quickly, so that the pattern-makers can, in turn, move quickly to make the preproduction parts. With computerization, Samhongsa can now e-mail information directly to the client's home office for instant approval or modifications. Once the pilot unit has been built and approved by the buyer/importer, production can begin.

Among the many high-tech tools used by the design department are CADS (computer-aided design systems) with three-dimensional layout scans, computerized lathes, and automatic chemical milling machines. But even die-cast locomotives require precise hand labor to weld the hundreds of small parts and details. The MTH New York Central J-1e Hudson (1997) had more than 500 separate assembly steps.

The lost-wax process, the same process used to make original custom jewelry, is still used to make the smaller detailed brass parts. Because many projects are in production, the schedule has to be carefully planned to make the best use of both labor and machinery.

Samhongsa never originates a train project itself. Ideas for MTH features, such as the forced-air smoke units, originate at MTH in Maryland but are developed in Seoul. Of course, without Samhongsa's micro motors, there would be no miniature fan that propels the smoke up the engine's smokestack or exhaust vent.

SAMHONGSA, THE COMPANY

Wherever Se Yong Lee walks at Samhongsa, all standing employees bow in sincere respect to their president. Under his leadership, the company has grown to 520 employees—304 in the model train division alone.

There are now 6 new companies owned and operated by former Samhongsa employees in the model train division and 17 throughout the company. Called "Sosachanges," they are allowed to work as subcontractors. Samhongsa provides them with the space and tools to operate.

When asked if he might be concerned that they could leave and subcontract to Lionel—MTH's primary competition—Mr. Lee commented, "I don't really pay any attention. We are not a military academy, so there might be some 'Young Tigers' considering that option. It's a normal nature of life. If somebody walked out of Samhongsa five years ago or three years ago, our system has improved so much since then that they would not be able to compete with our present efficiency and speed."

In the late 1980s, when the Korean economy was booming, Samhongsa started recruiting potential workers from outlying rural high schools. Nearly 300 workers were hired in that manner. The company provided dormitory facilities and meals in the company cafeteria, and there was also a small company convenience store. The dormitory is gone now; the company instead takes jobs out into the countryside. In 1989 a second factory was completed in Choongnam province.

In 1992 Samhongsa expanded again by manufacturing pneumatic gas lifts/springs for chairs and exercise equipment and expanded yet again with

additional plants. In 1995 Samhongsa began operation of its motor factory in Shanghai, China. In 1996 it expanded its product line to include a personal hygiene product incorporating its developed technology with the Sanicleanet bidet. In 1997 it established Samhongsa Precision in Quindao Kyoju, China, in a 73,537-square-foot facility. Despite the expansions, the high-end products such as model trains are still manufactured in Seoul.

In December 1998 Samhongsa received its second Presidential Citation in the Grand Prize for Small and Medium Industries (the first was in 1986). It has also been ISO-9001 certified from KAITECH-KTL for its gas springs in 1996 and again in 1997 for its motors. It is currently working toward certification of three-rail model trains.

In 1997 the Korean currency, the Won, was devalued against the U.S. dollar, and the Korean economy, along with the rest of the Asian economy, took a quick dive. The International Monetary Fund (IMF) was called in to restructure Korean companies, but Samhongsa was going in the opposite direction—continuing to grow. It took its profits and reinvested in the company. "We were not involved with the old 'Chaebu' banking system, which was bad at the time," recalled Mr. Lee. "Before the IMF

came in, we had prepared for what was coming, and in 1992 restructured our system for the next five years." He continued, "We also have good customers who are friendly with us and will give us advance payments. It enabled us to take care of our subcontractors, which also put pressure on us to become more competitive."

Because the model train division of Samhongsa is totally dependent on export (the Korean market has no interest in model trains), the company has had to expand and has done so successfully, in other areas.

Although the model train division of Samhongsa is only one of four specialties of the company, miniature trains will continue to be the company's most recognized and novel product. You will probably never see the name "Samhongsa" on the box of a model train in the U.S. because, as Mr. Lee observed, "Our customers know more about marketing in the U.S. and Europe. We do our best as subcontractors who can concentrate on improving the product."

The relationship—and shared vision—between Samhongsa and MTH have made them a great success story. Together they are a formidable team that others in the American toy train industry are going to have to reckon with as the 20th century ends and the 21st century begins.

Premier Line
Steam Locomotives

Premier steam locomotives are accurate scale (1:48) models of specific prototype locomotives. Heavy, beautifully detailed, smooth-running models that are meant to look great on a shelf or a layout, Premier steam locomotives are the "top-of-the-line" offerings from M.T.H. Electric Trains. Premier steam locomotives come equipped with a variety of features such as die-cast boilers and tenders, die-cast trucks, constant-voltage lighting, electronic reversing, cab interiors including figures, firebox glow, smoke, and more. Proto-Sound is optional. Many of the models are available in two-rail DC versions.

Number 20-3030   2-8-8-4 Yellowstone Duluth, Missabe & Iron Range 227

20-3023 4-Truck Shay West Virginia Pulp & Paper Co. 12

20-3006 4-6-2 Southern Ps-4 1401

20-3007 4-6-2 USRA Heavy Pacific New York Central 4912

20-3008 4-6-2 USRA Heavy Pacific Santa Fe 3421

		MSRP	Current

Shay (4-Truck)
20–3023	West Virginia Pulp & Paper Co. 4-Truck Shay Steam Locomotive numbered 12 Black; 1997		
	(–1) 3-Rail w/ Proto-Sound	1,095	1,400
	(–2) 2-Rail	1,095	1,000

Berkshire (2-8-4)
20–3032	Nickel Plate 2-8-4 Berkshire Steam Locomotive Black/Silver/Gold; 1999		
	(–1) 3-Rail w/ Proto-Sound	900	CP
	(–2) 2-Rail	900	CP

Ten-Wheeler (4-6-0)
20–3031	Pennsylvania RR 4-6-0 G-5 Ten-Wheeler Steam Locomotive Black; 1999		
	(–1) 3-Rail w/ Proto-Sound	700	CP
	(–2) 2-Rail	700	CP

Pacific (4-6-2)
20–3005	Southern 4-6-2 Ps-4 Pacific Steam Locomotive Green/Silver; 1994		
	(–1) 3-Rail w/ Proto-Sound	899	1,200

		MSRP	Current
20–3006	Southern 4-6-2 Ps-4 Pacific Steam Locomotive numbered 1401 Green/Silver w/ Gold striping and Tuscan cab roof; 1994		
	(–1) 3-Rail w/ Proto-Sound	899	1,150
20–3007	New York Central 4-6-2 USRA Heavy Pacific Steam Locomotive numbered 4912 Black w/ Gray firebox and smokebox; 1994		
	(–1) 3-Rail w/ Proto-Sound	899	1,100
20–3008	Santa Fe 4-6-2 USRA Heavy Pacific Steam Locomotive numbered 3421 on Tender Black; 1994		
	(–1) 3-Rail w/ Proto-Sound	899	1,100
20–3018	Pennsylvania RR 4-6-2 K-4s Pacific Steam Locomotive Black; 1996		
	(–1) 3-Rail w/ Proto-Sound	899	1,450
	(–2) 2-Rail	899	1,150

20-3019 4-6-2 K-4s Pacific Pennsylvania 5495

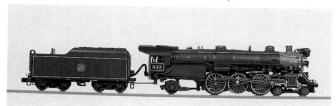
20-3028 4-6-2 Pacific Jersey Central *Blue Comet* 833

20-3016 4-6-4 Streamlined Hudson New York Central *Empire State Express* 5429

20-3020 4-6-4 J-1e Hudson New York Central 5344

20-3015 4-8-4 Northern Santa Fe 2921

		MSRP	Current
20–3019	Pennsylvania RR 4-6-2 K-4s Pacific Steam Locomotive numbered 5495 Black; 1996		
	(–1) 3-Rail w/ Proto-Sound	899	1,350
	(–2) 2-Rail	899	1,100
20–3028	Central RR of New Jersey 4-6-2 *Blue Comet* Pacific Steam Locomotive numbered 833 Blue; 1998		
	(–1) 3-Rail w/ Proto-Sound	900	1,100
	(–2) 2-Rail	900	950

Hudson (4-6-4)

		MSRP	Current
20–3016	New York Central 4-6-4 *Empire State Express* Streamlined Hudson Steam Locomotive numbered 5429 Black/Silver w/ disk-type drivers and bullet nose; 1995		
	(–1) 3-Rail w/ Proto-Sound	899	1,700
	(–2) 2-Rail	899	1,400
20–3020	New York Central 4-6-4 J-1e Hudson Steam Locomotive numbered 5344 Black; 1996		
	(–1) 3-Rail w/ Proto-Sound	899	1,300
	(–2) 2-Rail	899	1,300

		MSRP	Current
20–3034	Chicago & North Western 4-6-4 E-4 Streamlined Hudson Steam Locomotive Green; 1999		
	(–1) 3-Rail w/ Proto-Sound	900	CP
	(–2) 2-Rail		

Northern (4-8-4)

		MSRP	Current
20–3013	Santa Fe 4-8-4 Northern Steam Locomotive numbered 2904 on Tender Black; 1995		
	(–1) 3-Rail w/ Proto-Sound	999	1,550
	(–2) 2-Rail	999	1,220
20–3014	Santa Fe 4-8-4 Northern Steam Locomotive numbered 2913 on Tender Black; 1995		
	(–1) 3-Rail w/ Proto-Sound	999	1,400
	(–2) 2-Rail	999	1,100
20–3015	Santa Fe 4-8-4 Northern Steam Locomotive numbered 2921 on Tender Black; 1995		
	(–1) 3-Rail w/ Proto-Sound	999	1,400
	(–2) 2-Rail	999	1,100

20-3024 4-8-4 Northern J Norfolk & Western 611

20-3029 4-8-4 GS-4 Northern Southern Pacific 4449

20-3017 2-6-6-6 Allegheny Chesapeake & Ohio 1604

	MSRP	Current

20–3024* Norfolk & Western 4-8-4 Northern J Steam Locomotive
numbered 611. *Reviewed in CTT November 1996*
Black; 1997

	MSRP	Current
(–1) 3-Rail w/ Proto-Sound	999	1,200
(–2) 2-Rail	999	1,000

20–3029* Southern Pacific 4-8-4 GS-4 Northern Steam Locomotive
numbered 4449. *Reviewed in CTT September 1999*
Black/Orange/Red; 1998

	MSRP	Current
(–1) 3-Rail w/ Proto-Sound	1,000	1,200
(–2) 2-Rail	1,000	1,000

20–3035 Chesapeake & Ohio 4-8-4 J-3 Greenbrier Northern Steam
Locomotive
Black; 1999

	MSRP	Current
(–1) 3-Rail w/ Proto-Sound	900	CP
(–2) 2-Rail	900	CP

Allegheny (2-6-6-6)

	MSRP	Current

20–3017 Chesapeake & Ohio 2-6-6-6 Allegheny Steam Locomotive
numbered 1604
Black w/ White striping; 1996

	MSRP	Current
(–1) 3-Rail w/ Proto-Sound	1,395	2,700
(–2) 2-Rail	1,395	2,700

Mallet (2-8-8-2)

20–3009 Norfolk & Western 2-8-8-2 Y6b Mallet Steam Locomotive
numbered 2197
Black w/ Gray smokebox; 1995

	MSRP	Current
(–1) 3-Rail w/ Proto-Sound	1,295	2,550
(–2) 2-Rail	1,295	2,000

20–3010 Baltimore & Ohio 2-8-8-2 Y3 Mallet Steam Locomotive
numbered 7032
Black; 1995

	MSRP	Current
(–1) 3-Rail w/ Proto-Sound	1,295	2,300

20–3011 Pennsylvania RR 2-8-8-2 Y3 Mallet Steam Locomotive
numbered 374
Black; 1995

	MSRP	Current
(–1) 3-Rail w/ Proto-Sound	1,295	2,500

20-3009   2-8-8-2 Y6b Mallet Norfolk & Western 2197

20-3010   2-8-8-2 Y3 Mallet Baltimore & Ohio 7032

20-3011   2-8-8-2 Y3 Mallet Pennsylvania 374

20-3012   2-8-8-2 Y3 Mallet Union Pacific 3670

		MSRP	Current
20–3012	Union Pacific 2-8-8-2 Y3 Mallet Steam Locomotive numbered 3670 Black w/ Gray firebox and smokebox; 1995		
	(–1) 3-Rail w/ Proto-Sound	1,295	2,300

Yellowstone (2-8-8-4)

20–3030	Duluth, Missabe & Iron Range 2-8-8-4 Yellowstone Steam Locomotive numbered 227 Black/Gray w/ White striping; 1999		
	(–1) 3-Rail w/ Proto-Sound	1,400	1,500
	(–2) 2-Rail	1,400	1,250

		MSRP	Current
Challenger (4-6-6-4)			
20–3000	Union Pacific 4-6-6-4 Challenger Steam Locomotive numbered 3982 Gray w/ Yellow striping; 1994		
	(–1) 3-Rail	1,295	2,600
20–3001	Union Pacific 4-6-6-4 Challenger Steam Locomotive numbered 3977 Gray w/ White striping; 1994		
	(–1) 3-Rail	1,295	2,500

20-3030 2-8-8-4 Yellowstone Duluth, Missabe & Iron Range 227

20-3000 4-6-6-4 Challenger Union Pacific (Yellow stripe) 3982

20-3001 4-6-6-4 Challenger Union Pacific (White stripe) 3977

20-3002 4-6-6-4 Challenger Union Pacific (Black) 3985

		MSRP	Current
20–3002	Union Pacific 4-6-6-4 Challenger Steam Locomotive numbered 3985 Black; 1994		
	(−1) 3-Rail	**1,295**	**3,000**
20–3003	Denver & Rio Grande Western 4-6-6-4 Challenger Steam Locomotive numbered 3800 Black w/ Gray firebox and White striping; 1994		
	(−1) 3-Rail	**1,295**	**2,600**
20–3004	Clinchfield RR 4-6-6-4 Challenger Steam Locomotive numbered 670 Black; 1994		
	(−1) 3-Rail	**1,295**	**2,800**

Cab-Forward (4-8-8-2)

		MSRP	Current
20–3025	Southern Pacific 4-8-8-2 AC-6 Cab-Forward Steam Locomotive numbered 4126 Black w/ Gray smokebox and White striping; 1998		
	(−1) 3-Rail w/ Proto-Sound	**1,400**	**1,500**
	(−2) 2-Rail	**1,400**	**1,350**

Big Boy (4-8-8-4)

		MSRP	Current
20–3021	Union Pacific 4-8-8-4 Big Boy Steam Locomotive numbered 4012 Black w/ Gray smokebox; 1997		
	(−1) 3-Rail w/ Proto-Sound	**1,395**	**2,500**
	(−2) 2-Rail	**1,395**	**2,000**

Auxiliary Water Tenders

		MSRP	Current
20–3022	Union Pacific Auxiliary Water Tender I Yellow; 1997	**199**	**360**

20-3003 4-6-6-4 Challenger Denver & Rio Grande Western 3800

20-3004 4-6-6-4 Challenger Clinchfield 670

20-3025 4-8-8-2 Cab-Forward Southern Pacific 4126

20-3021 4-8-8-4 Big Boy Union Pacific 4012

Top: 20-3022 Water Tender Union Pacific; **bottom left:** 20-3026 Water Tender Norfolk & Western, Maroon stripe for J Northern no. 20-3024; **bottom right:** 20-3027 Water Tender Norfolk & Western, Black for use with Y6b Mallet no. 20-3009

		MSRP	Current
20–3026	Norfolk & Western Auxiliary Water Tender II (box numbered 3126) Black w/ Maroon striping to match Norfolk & Western J Northern, no. 20-3024; 1998	200	235

		MSRP	Current
20-3027	Norfolk & Western Auxiliary Water Tender II (box numbered 3127) Black w/ Gold lettering to match Norfolk & Western Y6b Mallet, no. 20-3009; 1997	200	245

1:32 Scale Steam Locomotives (Consolidation 2-8-0)

20-5001	Southern Pacific 2-8-0 C-9 Consolidation Steam Locomotive (Electric) N/A; 1994	3,250	3,250
20-5002	Southern Pacific 2-8-0 C-9 Consolidation Steam Locomotive (Live Steam) N/A; 1994	3,300	3,300
20-5003	Southern Pacific 2-8-0 C-9 Consolidation Steam Locomotive (Live Steam Kit) N/A; 1994	2,800	2,800

Premier Line
Diesel & Electric Locomotives

Premier diesel locomotives, like their steam counterparts, are accurate scale (1:48) models of prototype locomotives. Their ABS bodies are handsomely decorated in a wide variety of roadnames, the models are nicely detailed, and they run well. Premier diesel locomotives make colorful additions to a collection, but they also perform well under operating conditions. Many features are standard (die-cast trucks, directional headlights, illuminated marker lights, metal chassis, etc.) and more are added with each new release. Proto-Sound is optional. Many models are available in two-rail DC versions.

Number 20-2185 Gas-Turbine Locomotive Union Pacific 75

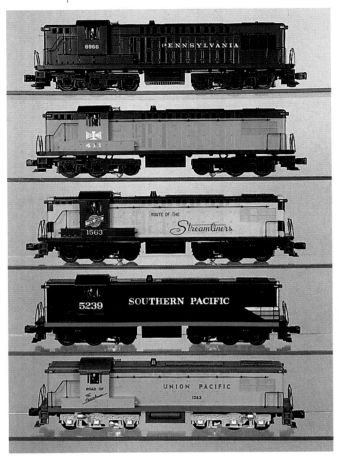

Premier Line AS-616s: top to bottom
20-2133-1 AS-616 Pennsylvania RR 8966
20-2134-1 AS-616 Bessemer & Lake Erie 411
20-2136-1 AS-616 Chicago & North Western 1563
20-2137-1 AS-616 Southern Pacific 5239
20-2138-1 AS-616 Union Pacific 1263

Premier Line BL2s: top to bottom
20-2130-1 BL2 Florida East Coast 606
20-2131-1 BL2 Monon 33
20-2132-1 BL2 Electro-Motive Division Demonstrator 497

AS-616

		MSRP	Current
20–2133	Pennsylvania RR AS-616 Diesel Locomotive numbered 8966 Brunswick Green; 1996		
	(−0) 3-Rail w/ Horn	299	375
	(−1) 3-Rail w/ Proto-Sound	379	450
	(−2) 2-Rail	299	375
20–2134	Bessemer & Lake Erie AS-616 Diesel Locomotive numbered 411 Orange; 1996		
	(−0) 3-Rail w/ Horn	299	300
	(−1) 3-Rail w/ Proto-Sound	379	325
	(−2) 2-Rail	299	300

		MSRP	Current
20–2135	SOO Line AS-616 Diesel Locomotive White/Red; 1996		
	(−0) 3-Rail w/ Horn	299	250
	(−1) 3-Rail w/ Proto-Sound	379	300
	(−2) 2-Rail	299	250
20–2136	Chicago & North Western AS-616 Diesel Locomotive numbered 1563 Yellow/Green; 1996		
	(−0) 3-Rail w/ Horn	299	300
	(−1) 3-Rail w/ Proto-Sound	379	390
	(−2) 2-Rail	299	300
20–2137	Southern Pacific AS-616 Diesel Locomotive numbered 5239 Black; 1996		
	(−0) 3-Rail w/ Horn	299	275
	(−1) 3-Rail w/ Proto-Sound	379	350
	(−2) 2-Rail	299	275
20–2138	Union Pacific AS-616 Diesel Locomotive numbered 1263 Yellow; 1996		
	(−0) 3-Rail w/ Horn	299	325
	(−1) 3-Rail w/ Proto-Sound	379	375
	(−2) 2-Rail	299	325

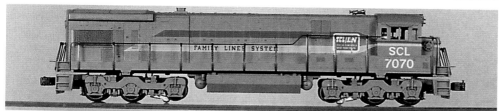

20-2016 C30-7 Louisville & Nashville
"Family Lines System" 7070

20-2017 C30-7 Union Pacific 2460

		MSRP	Current

BL2

20–2129 Western Maryland BL2 Diesel Locomotive
Black; 1996

	MSRP	Current
(–0) 3-Rail w/ Horn	299	225
(–1) 3-Rail w/ Proto-Sound	379	300
(–2) 2-Rail	299	225

20–2130 Florida East Coast BL2 Diesel Locomotive numbered 606
Red/Yellow; 1996

	MSRP	Current
(–0) 3-Rail w/ Horn	299	275
(–1) 3-Rail w/ Proto-Sound	379	350
(–2) 2-Rail	299	275

20–2131 Monon BL2 Diesel Locomotive numbered 33
Brown; 1996

	MSRP	Current
(–0) 3-Rail w/ Horn	299	375
(–1) 3-Rail w/ Proto-Sound	379	375
(–2) 2-Rail	299	300

20–2132 Electro-Motive Division BL2 Demonstrator Diesel
Locomotive numbered 497
Lt. Blue/Yellow; 1996

	MSRP	Current
(–0) 3-Rail w/ Horn	299	300
(–1) 3-Rail w/ Proto-Sound	379	375
(–2) 2-Rail	299	300

C30-7

20–2010 Burlington Northern C30-7 Diesel Locomotive numbered
5005
Green/Black; 1994

	MSRP	Current
(–0) 3-Rail w/ Horn	279	400
(–1) 3-Rail w/ Proto-Sound	349	475
(–2) 2-Rail	279	400

20–2011 Conrail C30-7 Diesel Locomotive
Blue/White; 1994

	MSRP	Current
(–0) 3-Rail w/ Horn	279	350
(–1) 3-Rail w/ Proto-Sound	349	290
(–2) 2-Rail	279	290

20–2012 CSX C30-7 Diesel Locomotive
Gray/Blue; 1994

	MSRP	Current
(–0) 3-Rail w/ Horn	279	300
(–1) 3-Rail w/ Proto-Sound	349	400
(–2) 2-Rail	279	300

20–2013 Norfolk Southern C30-7 Diesel Locomotive
Black/White; 1994

	MSRP	Current
(–0) 3-Rail w/ Horn	279	350
(–1) 3-Rail w/ Proto-Sound	349	425
(–2) 2-Rail	279	350

20–2014 Norfolk & Western C30-7 Diesel Locomotive
Red/Yellow; 1994

	MSRP	Current
(–0) 3-Rail w/ Horn	279	350
(–1) 3-Rail w/ Proto-Sound	349	425
(–2) 2-Rail	279	350

20–2015 Santa Fe C30-7 Diesel Locomotive
Blue/Yellow; 1994

	MSRP	Current
(–0) 3-Rail w/ Horn	279	275
(–1) 3-Rail w/ Proto-Sound	349	350
(–2) 2-Rail	279	275

20–2016 Louisville & Nashville C30-7 Diesel Locomotive numbered
7070
Gray/Red "Family Lines System" scheme; 1994

	MSRP	Current
(–0) 3-Rail w/ Horn	279	325
(–1) 3-Rail w/ Proto-Sound	349	400
(–2) 2-Rail	279	325

20–2017 Union Pacific C30-7 Diesel Locomotive numbered 2460
Yellow/Gray; 1994

	MSRP	Current
(–0) 3-Rail w/ Horn	279	350
(–1) 3-Rail w/ Proto-Sound	349	425
(–2) 2-Rail	279	350

20-2171 Amtrak Dash 8-40B 509

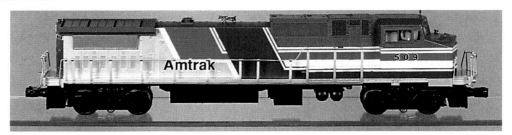

		MSRP	Current

Dash 8-40

20–2001 Union Pacific Dash 8-40C Diesel Locomotive
Gray/Yellow; 1993

		MSRP	Current
(–0) 3-Rail w/ Horn		249	300
(–2) 2-Rail		249	250

20–2002 Norfolk Southern Dash 8-40C Diesel Locomotive
Black/White; 1993

		MSRP	Current
(–0) 3-Rail w/ Horn		249	300
(–2) 2-Rail		249	250

20–2003 Burlington Northern Dash 8-40C Diesel Locomotive
Green/Black/White; 1993

		MSRP	Current
(–0) 3-Rail w/ Horn		249	300
(–2) 2-Rail		249	250

20–2004 Conrail Dash 8-40C Diesel Locomotive numbered 6050
Blue/White; 1993

		MSRP	Current
(–0) 3-Rail w/ Horn		249	250
(–2) 2-Rail		249	250

20–2005 Chicago & North Western Dash 8-40C Diesel Locomotive
Yellow/Green; 1993

		MSRP	Current
(–0) 3-Rail w/ Horn		249	400
(–2) 2-Rail		249	300

20–2006* CSX Dash 8-40C Diesel Locomotive numbered 7599.
Reviewed in CTT November 1993
Gray/Blue; 1993

		MSRP	Current
(–0) 3-Rail w/ Horn		249	425
(–2) 2-Rail		249	425

20–2007 Amtrak Dash 8-40B Diesel Locomotive numbered 500
Red/White/Blue; 1993

		MSRP	Current
(–0) 3-Rail w/ Horn		249	500
(–2) 2-Rail		249	300

20–2008 Santa Fe Dash 8-40C Diesel Locomotive numbered 804
Silver/Red; 1993

		MSRP	Current
(–0) 3-Rail w/ Horn		249	600
(–2) 2-Rail		249	300

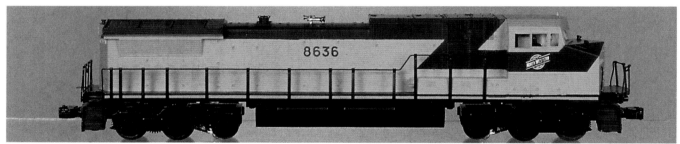

20-2159 Dash 9 Chicago & North Western 8636

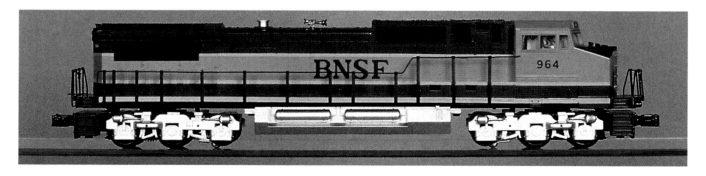

20-2179 Dash 9 Burlington Northern Santa Fe 964 (from boxed set)

20-2178 DD40AX Union Pacific 6922

	MSRP	Current
20–2009 Santa Fe Dash 8-40B Diesel Locomotive Silver/Red; 1993		
(–) 3-Rail w/ Horn	249	450
20–2171 Amtrak Dash 8-40B Diesel Locomotive numbered 509 Red/Blue/Silver; 1998		
(–1) 3-Rail w/ Proto-Sound	400	400

Dash 9

	MSRP	Current
20–2159 Chicago & North Western Dash 9 Diesel Locomotive numbered 8636 Yellow/Green; 1997		
(–1) 3-Rail w/ Proto-Sound	399	350
(–2) 2-Rail	299	300
20–2160 General Electric Dash 9 Demonstrator Diesel Locomotive numbered 2002 Red/Silver/Blue; 1997		
(–1) 3-Rail w/ Proto-Sound	399	350
(–2) 2-Rail	299	300
20–2172 Burlington Northern Santa Fe Dash 9 Diesel Locomotive numbered 972 (separate sale) Green/Orange; 1998		
(–1) 3-Rail w/ Proto-Sound	400	450
20–2179 Burlington Northern Santa Fe Diesel Locomotive from Boxed Set no. 2 Dash 9 Unit Train numbered 964 Green/Yellow; 1998		
(–) 3-Rail w/ Proto-Sound	600	600

DD40AX

	MSRP	Current
20–2178 Union Pacific DD40AX Diesel Locomotive numbered 6900 and 6922 Yellow; 1998		
(–1) 3-Rail w/ Proto-Sound	600	850

DR-12-8-1500 "Centipede"

	MSRP	Current
20–2200 Pennsylvania RR Centipede AA Diesel Locomotive Set Green/Gold; 1999		
(–1) 3-Rail w/ Proto-Sound	700	CP
(–2) 2-Rail	700	CP

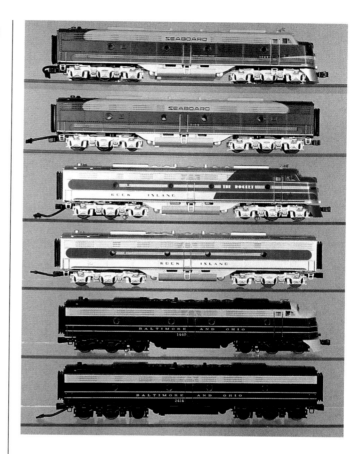

Premier Line E8s: top to bottom
20-2168 E8 ABA Seaboard 3049, 3105 (dummy A 3050 not pictured)
20-2169 E8 ABA Rock Island (dummy A not pictured)
20-2170 E8 ABA Baltimore & Ohio 1440, 2414 (dummy A 1414 not pictured)

E8

	MSRP	Current
20–2168 Seaboard E8 ABA Diesel Locomotive Set numbered 3049, 3105, and 3050 Green/Yellow/Orange lettered "Orange Blossom Special"; 1997		
(–1) 3-Rail w/ Proto-Sound	699	750
(–2) 2-Rail	629	630

Premier Line F3 A's: left to right, top to bottom
20-2051 F3 AA Denver & Rio Grande 5524, 20-2052 F3 AA Florida East Coast 502
20-2055 F3 AA Union Pacific 1449, 20-2057 F3 AA Canadian Pacific 4002

		MSRP	Current
20–2169	Rock Island E8 ABA Diesel Locomotive Set Red/Silver lettered "The Rocket"; 1997		
	(−1) 3-Rail w/ Proto-Sound	699	900
	(−2) 2-Rail	629	700
20–2170	Baltimore & Ohio E8 ABA Diesel Locomotive Set numbered 1440, 2414, and 1414 Blue/Gray/Black; 1997		
	(−1) 3-Rail	699	750
	(−2) 2-Rail	629	630
20–2205	Pere Marquette E8 ABA Diesel Locomotive Set Blue/Yellow lettered "Chesapeake and Ohio"; 1999		
	(−1) 3-Rail w/ Proto-Sound	650	CP
20–2206	Electro-Motive Division E8 ABA Diesel Locomotive Set Lt. Blue/Silver; 1999		
	(−1) 3-Rail w/ Proto-Sound	650	CP
20–2207	Kansas City Southern E8 ABA Diesel Locomotive Set Yellow/Red; 1999		
	(−1) 3-Rail	650	CP
20–2208	Union Pacific E8 ABA Diesel Locomotive Set Yellow; 1999		
	(−1) 3-Rail	650	CP

F3 ABA

		MSRP	Current
20–2153	Santa Fe *El Capitan* (F3 ABA Diesel Locomotive) Boxed Set (box numbered 30-2153); also includes Railway Express Agency car no. 3430, coach 3103, dome 500, and observation 3198 Silver/Red; 1997		
	(−1) 3-Rail w/ Proto-Sound	939	1,300

		MSRP	Current
20–2176	New York Central F3 ABA Diesel Locomotive Set Two-tone Gray/White; 1998		
	(−1) 3-Rail w/ Proto-Sound	680	725
20–2177	Southern F3 ABA Diesel Locomotive Set Green/White; 1998		
	(−1) 3-Rail w/ Proto-Sound	680	725
20–2198	Reading F3 ABA Diesel Locomotive Set Green; 1999		
	(−1) 3-Rail w/ Proto-Sound	600	CP
20–2199	Southern Pacific F3 ABA Diesel Locomotive Set Red/Orange; 1999		
	(−1) 3-Rail w/ Proto-Sound	600	CP

F3 AA

		MSRP	Current
20–2050	Baltimore & Ohio F3 AA Diesel Locomotive Set Blue/Gray; 1994		
	(−0) 3-Rail w/ Horn	399	1,050
	(−1) 3-Rail w/ Proto-Sound	485	1,150
	(−2) 2-Rail	399	1,050
20–2051	Denver & Rio Grande Western F3 AA Diesel Locomotive Set Yellow/Silver; 1994		
	(−0) 3-Rail w/ Horn	399	1,300
	(−1) 3-Rail w/ Proto-Sound	485	1,400
	(−2) 2-Rail	399	1,300
20–2052	Florida East Coast F3 AA Diesel Locomotive Set Red/Yellow; 1994		
	(−0) 3-Rail w/ Horn	399	1,300
	(−1) 3-Rail w/ Proto-Sound	485	1,400
	(−2) 2-Rail	399	1,300

		MSRP	Current
20–2053	Central RR of New Jersey F3 AA Diesel Locomotive Set Blue/Orange; 1994		
	(–0) 3-Rail w/ Horn	399	1,300
	(–1) 3-Rail w/ Proto-Sound	485	1,400
	(–2) 2-Rail	399	1,300
20–2054	Pennsylvania RR F3 AA Diesel Locomotive Set Tuscan Red w/ 5 Gold stripes; 1994		
	(–0) 3-Rail w/ Horn	399	825
	(–1) 3-Rail w/ Proto-Sound	485	925
	(–2) 2-Rail	399	825
20–2055	Union Pacific F3 AA Diesel Locomotive Set Yellow/Gray; 1994		
	(–0) 3-Rail w/ Horn	399	1,300
	(–1) 3-Rail w/ Proto-Sound	485	1,400
	(–2) 2-Rail	399	1,300
20–2056	Western Pacific F3 AA Diesel Locomotive Set Silver/Orange; 1994		
	(–0) 3-Rail w/ Horn	399	1,000
	(–1) 3-Rail w/ Proto-Sound	485	1,100
	(–2) 2-Rail	399	1,000
20–2057	Canadian Pacific F3 AA Diesel Locomotive Set Maroon/Gray; 1994		
	(–0) 3-Rail w/ Horn	399	850
	(–1) 3-Rail w/ Proto-Sound	485	950
	(–2) 2-Rail	399	850

		MSRP	Current
20–2083	Western Maryland F3 AA Diesel Locomotive Set Black; 1995		
	(–0) 3-Rail w/ Horn	399	650
	(–1) 3-Rail w/ Proto-Sound	485	750
	(–2) 2-Rail	399	650
20–2084*	Missouri-Kansas-Texas F3 AA Diesel Locomotive Set numbered 201A and 201C. *Reviewed in CTT December 1995* Red/White; 1995		
	(–0) 3-Rail w/ Horn	399	850
	(–1) 3-Rail w/ Proto-Sound	485	850
	(–2) 2-Rail	399	750
20–2085	Burlington F3 AA Diesel Locomotive Set Silver/Red; 1995		
	(–0) 3-Rail w/ Horn	399	1,125
	(–1) 3-Rail w/ Proto-Sound	485	1,125
	(–2) 2-Rail	399	1,050
20–2086	Lehigh Valley F3 AA Diesel Locomotive Set Red/Black; 1995		
	(–0) 3-Rail w/ Horn	399	700
	(–1) 3-Rail w/ Proto-Sound	485	700
	(–2) 2-Rail	399	625
20–2087	Northern Pacific F3 AA Diesel Locomotive Set Two-tone Green lettered "Main Street of the Northwest"; 1995		
	(–0) 3-Rail w/ Horn	399	575
	(–1) 3-Rail w/ Proto-Sound	485	675
	(–2) 2-Rail	399	575

20-2151 Santa Fe *El Capitan* Set, F3 AA
numbers 18 and 19, B unnumbered

20-2084 Missouri-Kansas-Texas F3 AA 201
and 201C
20-2084 Missouri-Kansas-Texas F3 B

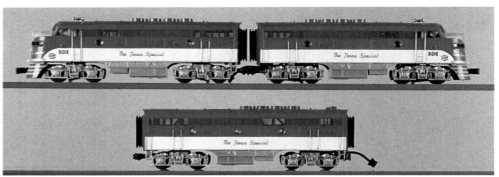

		MSRP	Current				MSRP	Current
20–2088	Atlantic Coast Line F3 AA Diesel Locomotive Set Purple/Silver; 1995				**20–2127**	Rock Island F3 AA Diesel Locomotive Set Red/Black; 1996		
	(**–0**) 3-Rail w/ Horn	399	1,000			(**–0**) 3-Rail w/ Horn	399	500
	(**–1**) 3-Rail w/ Proto-Sound	485	1,100			(**–1**) 3-Rail w/ Proto-Sound	485	575
	(**–2**) 2-Rail	399	1,000			(**–2**) 2-Rail	399	500
20–2089	New Haven F3 AA Diesel Locomotive Set Black/Orange; 1995				**20–2128**	Alaska RR F3 AA Diesel Locomotive Set Blue/Yellow; 1996		
	(**–0**) 3-Rail w/ Horn	399	675			(**–0**) 3-Rail w/ Horn	399	575
	(**–1**) 3-Rail w/ Proto-Sound	485	675			(**–1**) 3-Rail w/ Proto-Sound	485	650
	(**–2**) 2-Rail	399	600			(**–2**) 2-Rail	399	575
20–2090	Electro-Motive Division F3 AA Demonstrator Diesel Locomotive Set Blue/White; 1995				**20–2151**	Santa Fe F3 AA Diesel Locomotive Set numbered 18 and 19 (from Boxed Set 20-2153) Silver/Red; 1997		
	(**–0**) 3-Rail w/ Horn	399	1,450			(**–1**) 3-Rail w/ Proto-Sound	485	550
	(**–1**) 3-Rail w/ Proto-Sound	485	1,550		**20–2152**	Louisville & Nashville F3 AA Diesel Locomotive Set Blue/Cream; 1997		
	(**–2**) 2-Rail	399	1,450			(**–1**) 3-Rail w/ Proto-Sound	485	650
20–2125	Chesapeake & Ohio F3 AA Diesel Locomotive Set Blue/Gray; 1996				**F3 B**			
	(**–0**) 3-Rail w/ Horn	399	650		**20–2050**	Baltimore & Ohio F3 B Unit Blue/Gray; 1998		
	(**–1**) 3-Rail w/ Proto-Sound	399	650			(**–3**) 3-Rail powered	230	300
	(**–2**) 2-Rail	399	575					
20–2126	Boston & Maine F3 AA Diesel Locomotive Set Red/Yellow; 1996				**20–2051**	Denver & Rio Grande Western F3 B Unit Yellow/Silver; 1998		
	(**–0**) 3-Rail w/ Horn	399	450			(**–3**) 3-Rail powered	230	300
	(**–1**) 3-Rail w/ Proto-Sound	485	550					
	(**–2**) 2-Rail	399	450					

Premieer Line F3 Bs: left to right, top to bottom

20-2050 F3 B Baltimore & Ohio, 20-2053 F3 B Jersey Central

20-2054 F3 B Pennsylvania RR 9501B (Tuscan), 20-2056 F3 B Western Pacific

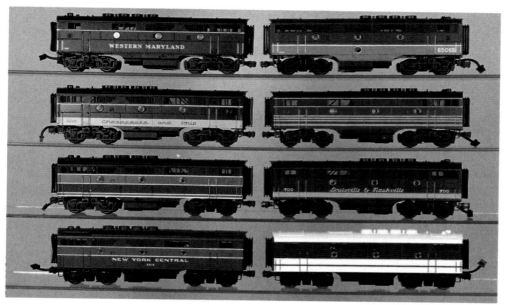

Premier Line F3 Bs: left to right, top to bottom

20-2083 F3 B Western Maryland 406, 20-2087 F3 B Northern Pacific 6506B 20-2125B F3 B Chesapeake & Ohio 8505, 20-2126B F3 B Boston & Maine 20-2127B F3 B Rock Island, 20-2152 F3 B Louisville & Nashville 700 20-2176 F3 B New York Central 2414 (from ABA set), 20-2177 F3 B Southern (from ABA set)

		MSRP	Current				MSRP	Current
20–2052	Florida East Coast F3 B Unit Red/Yellow; 1998				20–2058	Baltimore & Ohio F3 B Unit Blue/White; 1994		
	(–3) 3-Rail powered	230	350			(–2) 2-Rail	149	300
						(–3) 3-Rail	149	300
20–2053	Central RR of New Jersey F3 B Unit Blue/Orange; 1998				20–2059	Denver & Rio Grande Western F3 B Unit Yellow/Silver; 1994		
	(–3) 3-Rail powered	230	300			(–2) 2-Rail	149	300
						(–3) 3-Rail	149	300
20–2054	Pennsylvania RR F3 B Unit numbered 9501B Tuscan Red w/ 5 Gold stripes; 1998				20–2060	Florida East Coast F3 B Unit Red/Yellow; 1994		
	(–3) 3-Rail powered	230	300			(–2) 2-Rail	149	350
						(–3) 3-Rail	149	350
20–2055	Union Pacific F3 B Unit Yellow/Gray; 1998				20–2061	Central RR of New Jersey F3 B Unit Blue/Orange; 1994		
	(–3) 3-Rail powered	230	220			(–2) 2-Rail	149	300
20–2056	Western Pacific F3 B Unit Silver/Orange; 1998					(–3) 3-Rail	149	300
	(–3) 3-Rail powered	230	300					
20–2057	Canadian Pacific F3 B Unit Maroon/Gray; 1998							
	(–3) 3-Rail powered	230	300					

20-2147 F40PH Amtrak 300

		MSRP	Current
20–2062	Pennsylvania RR F3 B Unit Tuscan; 1994		
	(**–2**) 2-Rail	**149**	**300**
	(**–3**) 3-Rail	**149**	**300**
20–2063	Union Pacific F3 B Unit Yellow/Gray; 1994		
	(**–2**) 2-Rail	**149**	**300**
	(**–3**) 3-Rail	**149**	**300**
20–2064	Western Pacific F3 B Unit Silver/Orange; 1994		
	(**–2**) 2-Rail	**149**	**300**
	(**–3**) 3-Rail	**149**	**300**
20–2065	Canadian Pacific F3 B Unit Maroon/Gray; 1994		
	(**–2**) 2-Rail	**149**	**300**
	(**–3**) 3-Rail	**149**	**300**
20–2083	Western Maryland F3 B Unit numbered 406 Black; 1998		
	(**–3**) 3-Rail powered	**230**	**230**
20–2084	Missouri-Kansas-Texas F3 B Unit Red/White; 1998		
	(**–3**) 3-Rail powered	**230**	**230**
20–2085	Burlington F3 B Unit Silver/Red; 1998		
	(**–3**) 3-Rail powered	**230**	**275**
20–2086	Lehigh Valley F3 B Unit Red/Black; 1998		
	(**–3**) 3-Rail powered	**230**	**230**
20–2087	Northern Pacific F3 B Unit numbered 6506B Two-tone Green lettered "Main Street of the Northwest"; 1998		
	(**–3**) 3-Rail powered	**230**	**220**
20–2088	Atlantic Coast Line F3 B Unit Purple/Silver; 1998		
	(**–3**) 3-Rail powered	**230**	**230**

		MSRP	Current
20–2089	New Haven F3 B Unit Black/Orange; 1998		
	(**–3**) 3-Rail powered	**230**	**230**
20–2090	Electro-Motive Division F3 Demonstrator B Unit Blue/White; 1998		
	(**–3**) 3-Rail powered	**230**	**330**
20–2091	Western Maryland F3 B Unit Black; 1995		
	(**–0**) 3-Rail	**159**	**150**
	(**–2**) 2-Rail	**159**	**150**
20–2092	Missouri-Kansas-Texas F3 B Unit Red/Silver; 1995		
	(**–2**) 2-Rail	**159**	**150**
	(**–3**)	**159**	**150**
20–2093	Burlington F3 B Unit Silver/Red; 1995		
	(**–2**) 2-Rail	**159**	**175**
	(**–3**)	**159**	**175**
20–2094	Lehigh Valley F3 B Unit Red/Black; 1995		
	(**–2**) 2-Rail	**159**	**150**
	(**–3**)	**159**	**150**
20–2095	Northern Pacific F3 B Unit Green; 1995		
	(**–2**) 2-Rail	**159**	**200**
	(**–3**)	**159**	**200**
20–2096	Atlantic Coast Line F3 B Unit Purple/Silver; 1995		
	(**–2**) 2-Rail	**159**	**150**
	(**–3**)	**159**	**150**
20–2097	New Haven F3 B Unit Black/Orange; 1995		
	(**–2**) 2-Rail	**159**	**150**
	(**–3**)	**159**	**150**

Premier Line FP45s: top to bottom
20-2143 FP45 Susquehanna 3636
20-2144 FP45 Burlington Northern 6622
20-2145 FP45 Santa Fe 5942

		MSRP	Current
20–2098	Electro-Motive Division F3 Demonstrator B Unit Blue/White; 1995		
	(–2) 2-Rail	159	350
	(–3)	159	350
20–2125	Chesapeake & Ohio F3 B Unit Blue/Gray; 1999		
	(–4) 3-Rail powered	230	CP
20–2125B	Chesapeake & Ohio F3 B Unit numbered 8505 Blue/Gray; 1996		
	(–3) 3-Rail	159	150
20–2126	Boston & Maine F3 B Unit Red/Yellow; 1999		
	(–4) 3-Rail powered	230	CP
20–2126B	Boston & Maine F3 B Unit Red/Yellow; 1996		
	(–3) 3-Rail	159	150

		MSRP	Current
20–2127	Rock Island F3 B Unit Red/Black; 1999		
	(–4) 3-Rail powered	230	CP
20–2127B	Rock Island F3 B Unit Red/Black; 1996		
	(–3) 3-Rail	159	150
20–2128	Alaska RR F3 B Unit Blue/Yellow; 1999		
	(–4) 3-Rail powered	230	CP
20–2128B	Alaska RR F3 B Unit Blue/Yellow; 1996		
	(–3) 3-Rail	159	150
20–2151	Santa Fe F3 B Unit (from Boxed Set 20-2153) Silver/Red; 1997		
	(–3) 3-Rail	159	300
20–2151	Santa Fe F3 B Unit Silver/Red; 1999		
	(–4) 3-Rail powered	230	300
20–2152	Louisville & Nashville F3 B Unit Blue/Cream; 1997		
	(–3) 3-Rail	159	250
20–2152	Louisville & Nashville F3 B Unit Blue/Cream; 1999		
	(–4) 3-Rail powered	230	CP

F40PH

		MSRP	Current
20–2147	Amtrak F40PH Diesel Locomotive numbered 300 Silver; 1997		
	(–1) 3-Rail w/ Proto-Sound	379	400
	(–2) 2-Rail	299	325

20-2146 FP45 Electro-Motive Division Demonstrator 169

20-2124 Union Pacific Gas-Turbine
Locomotive 5 and 5B (with Tender)

		MSRP	Current
20–2148	Massachusetts Bay F40PH Diesel Locomotive Purple/Silver; 1997		
	(–1) 3-Rail w/ Proto-Sound	380	375
	(–2) 2-Rail	300	300
20–2149	Metra F40PH Diesel Locomotive Blue/Orange; 1997		
	(–1) 3-Rail w/ Proto-Sound	380	375
	(–2) 2-Rail	300	300
20–2150	CalTran F40PH Diesel Locomotive Silver/Blue; 1997		
	(–1) 3-Rail w/ Proto-Sound	380	375
	(–2) 2-Rail	300	300

F59PH

20–2213	Amtrak F59PH Diesel Locomotive Silver/Blue; 1999		
	(–1) 3-Rail w/ Proto-Sound	330	CP

FP45

20–2143	Susquehanna FP45 Diesel Locomotive numbered 3636 Yellow/Green; 1997		
	(–1) 3-Rail w/ Proto-Sound	379	330
	(–2) 2-Rail	299	325

		MSRP	Current
20–2144	Burlington Northern FP45 Diesel Locomotive numbered 6622 and 6615 Green/Black; 1997		
	(–1) 3-Rail w/ Proto-Sound	379	300
	(–2) 2-Rail	299	300
20–2145	Santa Fe FP45 Diesel Locomotive numbered 5942 Blue/Yellow; 1997		
	(–1) 3-Rail w/ Proto-Sound	379	320
	(–2) 2-Rail	299	250
20–2146	Electro-Motive Division FP45 Demonstrator Diesel Locomotive numbered 169 and 218 Blue/White; 1997		
	(–1) 3-Rail w/ Proto-Sound	379	300
	(–2) 2-Rail	299	250

Gas/Coal-Turbine

20–2124	Union Pacific Gas-Turbine Locomotive numbered 5, 5B and Tender Yellow/Silver; 1996		
	(–1) 3-Rail w/ Proto-Sound	999	1,500
	(–2) 2-Rail	999	1,250
20–2185	Union Pacific Veranda Gas-Turbine Locomotive w/ Tender numbered 75 Yellow; 1998		
	(–1) 3-Rail w/ Proto-Sound	699	900
	(–2) 2-Rail	699	700

20-2185 Union Pacific Veranda Gas-
Turbine Locomotive 75 (with Tender)

20-2189 Amtrak Genesis 64

		MSRP	Current
20–2214	Union Pacific Coal-Turbine Locomotive numbered 80 Yellow; 1999		
	(−1) 3-Rail w/ Proto-Sound	**1,000**	**CP**

Genesis

		MSRP	Current
20–2189	Amtrak Genesis Diesel Locomotive numbered 64 Silver; 1998		
	(−1) 3-Rail w/ Proto-Sound	**330**	**400**

GP7

		MSRP	Current
20–2210	Pennsylvania RR GP7 Diesel Locomotive Brunswick Green; 1999		
	(−1) 3-Rail w/ Proto-Sound	**300**	**CP**
20–2211	Boston & Maine GP7 Diesel Locomotive Tuscan Red; 1999		
	(−1) 3-Rail w/ Proto-Sound	**300**	**CP**
20–2212	Great Northern GP7 Diesel Locomotive Orange/Green; 1999		
	(−1) 3-Rail w/ Proto-Sound	**300**	**CP**

GP9

		MSRP	Current
20–2033	New York Central GP9 Diesel Locomotive Gray/White; 1994		
	(−0) 3-Rail w/ Horn	**279**	**400**
	(−1) 3-Rail w/ Proto-Sound	**349**	**475**
	(−2) 2-Rail	**279**	**400**

		MSRP	Current
20–2034	Baltimore & Ohio GP9 Diesel Locomotive numbered 6604 Blue/White; 1994		
	(−0) 3-Rail w/ Horn	**279**	**450**
	(−1) 3-Rail w/ Proto-Sound	**349**	**525**
	(−2) 2-Rail	**279**	**450**
20–2035	Chicago & North Western GP9 Diesel Locomotive numbered 1716 Green/Yellow; 1994		
	(−0) 3-Rail w/ Horn	**279**	**400**
	(−1) 3-Rail w/ Proto-Sound	**349**	**475**
	(−2) 2-Rail	**279**	**400**
20–2036	Santa Fe GP9 Diesel Locomotive numbered 710 Blue/Yellow; 1994		
	(−0) 3-Rail w/ Horn	**279**	**300**
	(−1) 3-Rail w/ Proto-Sound	**349**	**375**
	(−2) 2-Rail	**279**	**300**
20–2037	Pennsylvania RR GP9 Diesel Locomotive Black/White; 1994		
	(−0) 3-Rail w/ Horn	**279**	**350**
	(−1) 3-Rail w/ Proto-Sound	**349**	**425**
	(−2) 2-Rail	**279**	**350**
20–2038	Union Pacific GP9 Diesel Locomotive Yellow/Gray; 1994		
	(−0) 3-Rail w/ Horn	**279**	**350**
	(−1) 3-Rail w/ Proto-Sound	**349**	**425**
	(−2) 2-Rail	**279**	**350**

Premmier Line GP9s: top to bottom
20-2040 GP9 Southern Pacific 5602
20-2034 GP9 Baltimore & Ohio 6604
20-2174 GP9 Texas & Pacific 1137
20-2175 GP9 Western Maryland 39

		MSRP	Current
20–2039	Southern GP9 Diesel Locomotive Green/White; 1994		
	(–0) 3-Rail w/ Horn	279	350
	(–1) 3-Rail w/ Proto-Sound	349	400
	(–2) 2-Rail	279	350
20–2040	Southern Pacific GP9 Diesel Locomotive numbered 5602 Black/Orange/Silver/Red "Black Widow" scheme; 1994		
	(–0) 3-Rail w/ Horn	279	400
	(–1) 3-Rail w/ Proto-Sound	349	475
	(–2) 2-Rail	279	400
20–2049	GP9 Diesel Locomotive Clear; 1995		
	(–1) 3-Rail w/ Proto-Sound	349	1,200
20–2173	Erie-Lackawanna GP9 Diesel Locomotive Gray/Maroon; 1998		
	(–1) 3-Rail w/ Proto-Sound	400	425

		MSRP	Current
20–2174	Texas & Pacific GP9 Diesel Locomotive numbered 1137 Gray/Blue; 1998		
	(–1) 3-Rail w/ Proto-Sound	400	425
20–2175	Western Maryland GP9 Diesel Locomotive numbered 39 and 35 Black; 1998		
	(–1) 3-Rail w/ Proto-Sound	400	425
20–2209	Lehigh Valley GP9 Diesel Locomotive Tuscan Red; 1999		
	(–1) 3-Rail w/ Proto-Sound	300	CP

GP20

		MSRP	Current
20–2139	Atlantic Coast Line GP20 Diesel Locomotive numbered 1029 and 1025 Black/Yellow; 1996		
	(–1) 3-Rail w/ Proto-Sound	379	300
	(–2) 2-Rail	299	300

Premier Line GP20s: top to bottom
20-2139 GP20 Atlantic Coast Line 1029
20-2140 GP20 Burlington Northern 2052
20-2141 GP20 Western Pacific 2007
20-2142 GP20 Electo-Motive Division
Demonstrator 5628

		MSRP	Current
20–2140	Burlington Northern GP20 Diesel Locomotive numbered 2052 Green; 1996		
	(–1) 3-Rail w/ Proto-Sound	379	400
	(–2) 2-Rail	299	350
20–2141	Western Pacific GP20 Diesel Locomotive numbered 2007 Silver/Orange; 1996		
	(–1) 3-Rail w/ Proto-Sound	379	400
	(–2) 2-Rail	299	300
20–2142	Electro-Motive Division GP20 Demonstrator Diesel Locomotive numbered 5628 Lt. Blue/Silver; 1996		
	(–1) 3-Rail w/ Proto-Sound	379	300
	(–2) 2-Rail	299	275

GP30

		MSRP	Current
20–2066	CSX GP30 Diesel Locomotive numbered 2320 Blue/Gray; 1995		
	(–0) 3-Rail w/ Horn	279	300
	(–1) 3-Rail w/ Proto-Sound	349	350
	(–2) 2-Rail	279	300
20–2067	Burlington Northern GP30 Diesel Locomotive Green/Black; 1995		
	(–0) 3-Rail w/ Horn	279	375
	(–1) 3-Rail w/ Proto-Sound	349	375
	(–2) 2-Rail	279	300
20–2068	Denver & Rio Grande Western GP30 Diesel Locomotive Black/Orange; 1995		
	(–0) 3-Rail w/ Horn	279	350
	(–1) 3-Rail w/ Proto-Sound	349	450
	(–2) 2-Rail	279	350

Premier Line GP 38-2s: left to right, top to bottom
20-2156 GP38-2 Southern Pacific 4800, 20-2157 GP38-2 Conrail 8265 20-2158 GP38-2 Gulf, Mobile & Ohio 740, 20-2186 GP38-2 Chessie System 3874 20-2187 GP38-2 Burlington Northern Santa Fe 2081, 20-2188 GP38-2 Union Pacific 2048

		MSRP	Current
20–2069	Union Pacific GP30 Diesel Locomotive Yellow/Red; 1995		
	(–0) 3-Rail w/ Horn	279	425
	(–1) 3-Rail w/ Proto-Sound	349	425
	(–2) 2-Rail	279	350
20–2070	Canadian Pacific GP30 Diesel Locomotive Maroon/Gray; 1995		
	(–0) 3-Rail w/ Horn	279	400
	(–1) 3-Rail w/ Proto-Sound	349	475
	(–2) 2-Rail	279	400
20–2071	Pennsylvania RR GP30 Diesel Locomotive Black/Yellow; 1995		
	(–0) 3-Rail	279	375
	(–1) 3-Rail w/ Proto-Sound	349	450
	(–2) 2-Rail	279	375
20–2072	Santa Fe GP30 Diesel Locomotive Blue/Yellow; 1995		
	(–0) 3-Rail w/ Horn	279	300
	(–1) 3-Rail w/ Proto-Sound	349	400
	(–2) 2-Rail	279	300
20–2073	Reading GP30 Diesel Locomotive Yellow/Green; 1995		
	(–0) 3-Rail w/ Horn	279	425
	(–1) 3-Rail w/ Proto-Sound	349	500
	(–2) 2-Rail	279	425
20–2074	GP30 Diesel Locomotive Clear; 1995		
	(–1) 3-Rail w/ Proto-Sound	349	1,500

GP38-2

		MSRP	Current
20–2156	Southern Pacific GP38-2 Diesel Locomotive numbered 4800 Gray/Red; 1997		
	(–1) 3-Rail w/ Proto-Sound	399	375
	(–2) 2-Rail	299	379
20–2157	Conrail GP38-2 Diesel Locomotive numbered 8265 Lt. Blue; 1997		
	(–1) 3-Rail w/ Proto-Sound	399	360
	(–2) 2-Rail	299	379
20–2158	GM&O GP38-2 Diesel Locomotive numbered 740 and 754 Red; 1997		
	(–1) 3-Rail w/ Proto-Sound	399	340
	(–2) 2-Rail	299	379
20–2186	Chessie System GP38-2 Diesel Locomotive numbered C&O 3874 Blue/Yellow; 1998		
	(–1) 3-Rail w/ Proto-Sound	299	300
20–2187	Burlington Northern Santa Fe GP38-2 Diesel Locomotive numbered 2081 and 2094 Orange/Green; 1998		
	(–1) 3-Rail w/ Proto-Sound	300	300
20–2188	Union Pacific GP38-2 Diesel Locomotive numbered 2048 and 2028 Yellow; 1998		
	(–1) 3-Rail w/ Proto-Sound	300	330

GP60M

		MSRP	Current
20–2180*	Santa Fe GP60M Diesel Locomotive numbered 157. **Reviewed in CTT January 1999* Silver/Red; 1998		
	(–1) 3-Rail w/ Proto-Sound	299	400

Premier Line H-10-44s: top to bottom
20-2075 H-10-44 Pennsylvania 8970
20-2082 H-10-44 Union Pacific 1265

		MSRP	Current
20–2181	Maersk GP60M Diesel Locomotive numbered 148 Lt. Blue/Silver; 1998		
	(−1) 3-Rail w/ Proto-Sound	299	400

H-10-44

		MSRP	Current
20–2075	Pennsylvania RR H-10-44 Diesel Locomotive numbered 8970 Black/Yellow; 1995		
	(−0) 3-Rail w/ Horn	279	450
	(−1) 3-Rail w/ Proto-Sound	349	450
	(−2) 2-Rail	279	375
20–2076	Frisco H-10-44 Diesel Locomotive Red/Gray; 1995		
	(−0) 3-Rail w/ Horn	279	400
	(−1) 3-Rail w/ Proto-Sound	349	400
	(−2) 2-Rail	279	300
20–2077	Santa Fe H-10-44 Diesel Locomotive Black/White; 1995		
	(−0) 3-Rail w/ Horn	279	450
	(−1) 3-Rail w/ Proto-Sound	349	450
	(−2) 2-Rail	279	375

		MSRP	Current
20–2078*	Chicago & North Western H-10-44 Diesel Locomotive numbered 1053. *Reviewed in CTT July 1995* Yellow/Green; 1995		
	(−0) 3-Rail w/ Horn	279	700
	(−1) 3-Rail w/ Proto-Sound	349	750
	(−2) 2-Rail	279	450
20–2079	New York Central H-10-44 Diesel Locomotive numbered 9108 Black; 1995		
	(−0) 3-Rail w/ Horn	279	450
	(−1) 3-Rail w/ Proto-Sound	349	450
	(−2) 2-Rail	279	375
20–2080	Milwaukee Road H-10-44 Diesel Locomotive Orange/Black; 1995		
	(−0) 3-Rail w/ Horn	279	575
	(−1) 3-Rail w/ Proto-Sound	349	575
	(−2) 2-Rail	279	500
20–2081	Southern Pacific H-10-44 Diesel Locomotive Black/Orange; 1995		
	(−0) 3-Rail w/ Horn	279	375
	(−1) 3-Rail w/ Proto-Sound	349	375
	(−2) 2-Rail	279	300

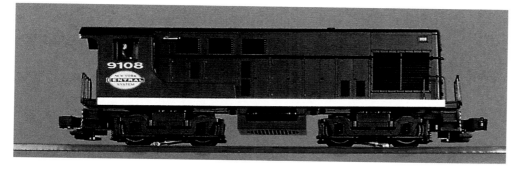

20-2079 F-M H-10-44 New York Central 9108

Premier Line H-24-66 Train Masters:
top to bottom
20-2122 H-24-66 Train Master Denver &
Rio Grande 565
20-2123 H-24-66 Train Master Santa Fe
2576
20-2182 H-24-66 Train Master Canadian
Pacific 8902

		MSRP	Current
20–2082	Union Pacific H-10-44 Diesel Locomotive numbered 1265 Yellow/Gray; 1995		
	(**–0**) 3-Rail w/ Horn	279	425
	(**–1**) 3-Rail w/ Proto-Sound	349	425
	(**–2**) 2-Rail	279	350

H-24-66 Train Master

		MSRP	Current
20–2120	Central RR of New Jersey Train Master Diesel Locomotive Blue/Orange; 1996		
	(**–0**) 3-Rail w/ Horn	279	375
	(**–1**) 3-Rail w/ Proto-Sound	349	450
20–2121	Southern Train Master Diesel Locomotive Green/Gray; 1996		
	(**–0**) 3-Rail w/ Horn	279	325
	(**–1**) 3-Rail w/ Proto-Sound	349	400
20–2122	Denver & Rio Grande Western Train Master Diesel Locomotive numbered 565 Orange/Gray; 1996		
	(**–0**) 3-Rail w/ Horn	279	450
	(**–1**) 3-Rail w/ Proto-Sound	349	450
20–2123	Santa Fe Train Master Diesel Locomotive numbered 2576 Silver/Red; 1996		
	(**–0**) 3-Rail w/ Horn	279	400
	(**–1**) 3-Rail w/ Proto-Sound	349	475

		MSRP	Current
20–2182	Fairbanks-Morse Train Master Demostrator Diesel Locomotive numbered TM-2 Red/Yellow; 1998		
	(**–1**) 3-Rail w/ Proto-Sound	299	400
20–2183	Canadian Pacific Train Master Diesel Locomotive numbered 8902 Gray/Maroon; 1998		
	(**–1**) 3-Rail w/ Proto-Sound	330	450
20–2201	Central RR of New Jersey Train Master Diesel Locomotive Orange/Blue; 1999		
	(**–1**) 3-Rail w/ Proto-Sound	330	CP
20–2202	Milwaukee Road Train Master Diesel Locomotive Black/Orange; 1999		
	(**–1**) 3-Rail w/ Proto-Sound	330	CP

PA-1

		MSRP	Current
20–2018	New York Central Alco PA AA Diesel Locomotive Set Gray/White; 1994		
	(**–0**) 3-Rail w/ Horn	479	700
	(**–1**) 3-Rail w/ Proto-Sound	549	800
	(**–2**) 2-Rail	479	700

		MSRP	Current
20–2019	Pennsylvania RR Alco PA AA Diesel Locomotive Set Tuscan; 1994		
	(–0) 3-Rail w/ Horn	479	700
	(–1) 3-Rail w/ Proto-Sound	549	800
	(–2) 2-Rail	479	700
20–2020	Southern Alco PA AA Diesel Locomotive Set Green/White; 1994		
	(–0) 3-Rail w/ Horn	479	500
	(–1) 3-Rail w/ Proto-Sound	549	600
	(–2) 2-Rail	479	500
20–2021	Union Pacific Alco PA AA Diesel Locomotive Set Yellow/Gray; 1994		
	(–0) 3-Rail w/ Horn	479	700
	(–1) 3-Rail w/ Proto-Sound	549	775
	(–2) 2-Rail	479	700
20–2022	Southern Pacific Alco PA AA Diesel Locomotive Set Red/Orange/Black; 1994		
	(–0) 3-Rail w/ Horn	479	550
	(–1) 3-Rail w/ Proto-Sound	549	650
	(–2) 2-Rail	479	550
20–2023	Wabash Alco PA AA Diesel Locomotive Set Blue/Gray; 1994		
	(–0) 3-Rail w/ Horn	479	625
	(–1) 3-Rail w/ Proto-Sound	549	700
	(–2) 2-Rail	479	625

		MSRP	Current
20–2024*	Santa Fe Alco PA AA Diesel Locomotive Set numbered 53 and 51. *Reviewed in CTT March 1995* Silver/Red; 1994		
	(–0) 3-Rail w/ Horn	479	750
	(–1) 3-Rail w/ Proto-Sound	549	850
	(–2) 2-Rail	479	750

PB-1

		MSRP	Current
20–2025	New York Central Alco PA B Unit Gray; 1994		
	(–0) 3-Rail	159	225
	(–2) 2-Rail	159	225
20–2026	Pennsylvania RR Alco PA B Unit Tuscan; 1994		
	(–0) 3-Rail	159	225
	(–2) 2-Rail	159	225
20–2027	Southern Alco PA B Unit Green/White; 1994		
	(–0) 3-Rail	159	200
	(–2) 2-Rail	159	200
20–2028	Union Pacific Alco PA B Unit Yellow/Gray; 1994		
	(–0) 3-Rail	159	225
	(–2) 2-Rail	159	225

		MSRP	Current
20–2029	Southern Pacific Alco PA B Unit Red/Orange; 1994		
	(–0) 3-Rail	159	200
	(–2) 2-Rail	159	200
20–2030	Wabash Alco PA B Unit Gray/Blue; 1994		
	(–0) 3-Rail	159	200
	(–2) 2-Rail	159	200
20–2031	Santa Fe Alco PA B Unit Silver/Red; 1994		
	(–0) 3-Rail	159	375
	(–2) 2-Rail	159	375
20–2032	Erie-Lackawanna Alco PA B Unit Gray/Maroon; 1994		
	(–0) 3-Rail	159	400

PA-1/PB-1

		MSRP	Current
20–2192	Nickel Plate Alco PA ABA Diesel Locomotive Set Green/White; 1999		
	(–1) 3-Rail w/ Proto-Sound	650	CP
20–2193	Lehigh Valley Alco PA ABA Diesel Locomotive Set Red; 1999		
	(–1) 3-Rail w/ Proto-Sound	650	CP
20–2194	Missouri-Kansas-Texas Alco PA ABA Diesel Locomotive Set Red/White/Yellow; 1999		
	(–1) 3-Rail w/ Proto-Sound	650	CP

RS-27

		MSRP	Current
20–2165	Penn Central RS-27 Diesel Locomotive numbered 2406 Black; 1997		
	(–1) 3-Rail w/ Proto-Sound	399	400
	(–2) 2-Rail	299	300
20–2166	Green Bay RS-27 Diesel Locomotive numbered 310 Red & Gray; 1997		
	(–1) 3-Rail w/ Proto-Sound	399	400
	(–2) 2-Rail	299	300

Premier Line RS-27s: top to bottom
20-2165 RS-27 Penn Central 2406
20-2166 RS-27 Green Bay & Western 310
20-2167 RS-27 Alco Demonstrator 640-5

		MSRP	Current
20–2167	Alco RS-27 Demonstrator Diesel Locomotive numbered 640-5 Purple/Gray; 1997		
	(–1) 3-Rail	399	400
	(–2) 2-Rail	299	300

SD9

		MSRP	Current
20–2108*	Chessie SD9 Diesel Locomotive numbered B&O 1831 and 1840. *Reviewed in CTT March 1996* Blue/Yellow; 1996		
	(–0) 3-Rail w/ Horn	299	600
	(–1) 3-Rail w/ Proto-Sound	379	600
	(–2) 2-Rail	299	500
20–2109	Pennsylvania RR SD9 Diesel Locomotive numbered 2618 Brunswick Green; 1996		
	(–0) 3-Rail w/ Horn	299	475
	(–1) 3-Rail w/ Proto-Sound	379	475
	(–2) 2-Rail	299	400

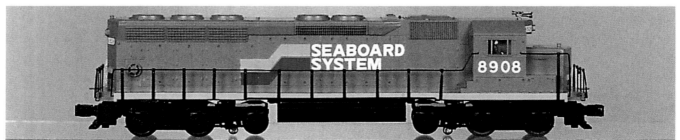

20-2102 SD45 Seaboard System 8908

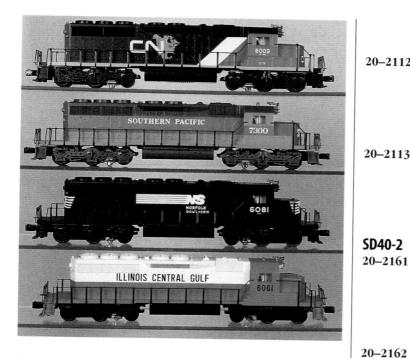

Premier Line SD40-2s: top to bottom
20-2161 SD40-2 Canadian National 6009
20-2162 SD40-2 Southern Pacific 7300
20-2163 SD40-2 Norfolk Southern 6081
20-2164 SD40-2 Illinois Central 6061

		MSRP	Current
20–2110	Nickel Plate SD9 Diesel Locomotive numbered 341 Black/Yellow; 1996		
	(**–0**) 3-Rail w/ Horn	299	400
	(**–1**) 3-Rail w/ Proto-Sound	379	400
	(**–2**) 2-Rail	299	350
20–2111	Burlington SD9 Diesel Locomotive numbered 325 Black/Green; 1996		
	(**–0**) 3-Rail w/ Horn	299	500
	(**–1**) 3-Rail w/ Proto-Sound	379	500
	(**–2**) 2-Rail	299	425

		MSRP	Current
20–2112	Southern Pacific SD9 Diesel Locomotive numbered 5360 Black/Silver; 1996		
	(**–0**) 3-Rail w/ Horn	299	450
	(**–1**) 3-Rail w/ Proto-Sound	379	450
	(**–2**) 2-Rail	299	400
20–2113	Denver & Rio Grande Western SD9 Diesel Locomotive Black/Yellow; 1996		
	(**–0**) 3-Rail w/ Horn	299	400
	(**–1**) 3-Rail w/ Proto-Sound	379	400
	(**–2**) 2-Rail	299	350

SD40-2

		MSRP	Current
20–2161	Canadian National SD40-2 Diesel Locomotive numbered 6009 Red/Black/White; 1997		
	(**–1**) 3-Rail	399	375
	(**–2**) 2-Rail	299	300
20–2162	Southern Pacific SD40-2 Diesel Locomotive numbered 7300 Red/Orange/Black; 1997		
	(**–1**) 3-Rail w/ Proto-Sound	399	375
20–2163	Norfolk Southern SD40-2 Diesel Locomotive numbered 6081 Black; 1997		
	(**–1**) 3-Rail w/ Proto-Sound	399	375
	(**–2**) 2-Rail	299	300
20–2164	Illinois Central SD40-2 Diesel Locomotive numbered 6061 and 6030 White/Orange; 1997		
	(**–1**) 3-Rail w/ Proto-Sound	399	425
	(**–2**) 2-Rail	299	300

SD45

		MSRP	Current
20–2100	Pennsylvania RR SD45 Diesel Locomotive Black; 1995		
	(**–0**) 3-Rail w/ Horn	299	400
	(**–1**) 3-Rail w/ Proto-Sound	379	475
	(**–2**) 2-Rail	299	400

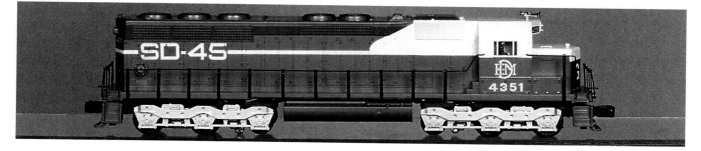

20-2107 SD45 Electro-Motive Division Demonstrator 4351

Premier Line SD60s: top to bottom
20-2115 SD60 Norfolk Southern 6694
20-2119 SD60 Electro-Motive Division Demonstrator 4

		MSRP	Current
20–2101	Reading SD45 Diesel Locomotive Green/Yellow; 1995		
	(–0) 3-Rail w/ Horn	299	350
	(–1) 3-Rail w/ Proto-Sound	379	425
	(–2) 2-Rail	299	350
20–2102	Seaboard System SD45 Diesel Locomotive numbered 8908 Gray/Yellow; 1995		
	(–0) 3-Rail w/ Horn	299	300
	(–1) 3-Rail w/ Proto-Sound	379	400
	(–2) 2-Rail	299	300
20–2103	Conrail SD45 Diesel Locomotive Blue/White; 1995		
	(–0) 3-Rail w/ Horn	299	300
	(–1) 3-Rail w/ Proto-Sound	379	400
	(–2) 2-Rail	299	300
20–2104	Great Northern SD45 Diesel Locomotive Green/Gold; 1995		
	(–0) 3-Rail w/ Horn	299	300
	(–1) 3-Rail w/ Proto-Sound	379	400
	(–2) 2-Rail	299	300
20–2105	Santa Fe SD45 Diesel Locomotive Red/Gold; 1995		
	(–0) 3-Rail w/ Horn	299	425
	(–1) 3-Rail w/ Proto-Sound	379	500
	(–2) 2-Rail	299	425

		MSRP	Current
20–2106	Union Pacific SD45 Diesel Locomotive Yellow/Black; 1995		
	(–0) 3-Rail w/ Horn	299	425
	(–1) 3-Rail w/ Proto-Sound	379	500
	(–2) 2-Rail	299	425
20–2107	Electro-Motive Division SD45 Demonstrator Diesel Locomotive numbered 4351 Metallic Blue/White; 1995		
	(–0) 3-Rail w/ Horn	299	500
	(–1) 3-Rail w/ Proto-Sound	379	575
	(–2) 2-Rail	299	500

SD60
20–2114	CSX SD60 Diesel Locomotive Blue/Gray; 1996		
	(–0) 3-Rail w/ Horn	299	400
	(–1) 3-Rail w/ Proto-Sound	379	400
	(–2) 2-Rail	299	325
20–2115	Norfolk Southern SD60 Diesel Locomotive numbered 6694 Black; 1996		
	(–0) 3-Rail w/ Horn	299	400
	(–1) 3-Rail w/ Proto-Sound	379	500
	(–2) 2-Rail	299	400
20–2116	Burlington Northern SD60 Diesel Locomotive Green/Black; 1996		
	(–0) 3-Rail w/ Horn	299	400
	(–1) 3-Rail w/ Proto-Sound	379	475
	(–2) 2-Rail	299	400

Premiere Line SD60Ms: top to bottom
20-2042 SD60M Norfolk Southern 6800
20-2044 SD60M Soo Line 6060

		MSRP	Current
20–2117	Chicago & North Western SD60 Diesel Locomotive Yellow/Green; 1996		
	(–0) 3-Rail w/ Horn	299	400
	(–1) 3-Rail w/ Proto-Sound	379	475
	(–2) 2-Rail	299	400
20–2118	Conrail SD60 Diesel Locomotive Blue/White; 1996		
	(–0) 3-Rail w/ Horn	299	350
	(–1) 3-Rail w/ Proto-Sound	379	425
	(–2) 2-Rail	299	350
20–2119	Electro-Motive Division SD60 Demonstrator Diesel Locomotive numbered Electro-Motive Division 4 Blue/Gray; 1996		
	(–0) 3-Rail w/ Horn	299	475
	(–1) 3-Rail w/ Proto-Sound	379	550
	(–2) 2-Rail	299	475
20–2041	Union Pacific SD60M Diesel Locomotive Yellow/Gray; 1994		
	(–0) 3-Rail w/ Horn	279	400
	(–1) 3-Rail w/ Proto-Sound	379	450
	(–2) 2-Rail	279	400
20–2042	Norfolk Southern SD60M Diesel Locomotive numbered 6800 Black; 1994		
	(–0) 3-Rail w/ Horn	279	400
	(–1) 3-Rail w/ Proto-Sound	349	450
	(–2) 2-Rail	279	400

		MSRP	Current
20–2043	Conrail SD60M Diesel Locomotive numbered 6867 Blue/White; 1994		
	(–0) 3-Rail w/ Horn	279	300
	(–1) 3-Rail w/ Proto-Sound	349	375
	(–2) 2-Rail	279	300
20–2044	SOO Line SD60M Diesel Locomotive numbered 6060 Red/White; 1994		
	(–0) 3-Rail w/ Horn	279	350
	(–1) 3-Rail w/ Proto-Sound	349	350
	(–2) 2-Rail	279	275
20–2045	Burlington Northern SD60M Diesel Locomotive Green/White; 1994		
	(–0) 3-Rail w/ Horn	279	300
	(–1) 3-Rail w/ Proto-Sound	349	400
	(–2) 2-Rail	279	300
20–2046	CSX SD60M Diesel Locomotive numbered 8711 Blue/White; 1994		
	(–0) 3-Rail w/ Horn	279	300
	(–1) 3-Rail w/ Proto-Sound	349	400
	(–2) 2-Rail	279	300
20–2047	Chicago & North Western SD60M Diesel Locomotive Yellow/Green; 1994		
	(–0) 3-Rail w/ Horn	279	475
	(–1) 3-Rail w/ Proto-Sound	349	475
	(–2) 2-Rail	279	400

20-2046 SD60M CSX 8711

20-2154 SD70MAC Burlington Northern
Santa Fe 9966

Premier Line EP-5s: top to bottom
20-2195 EP-5 New Haven 370
20-2196 EP-5 Great Northern 2357

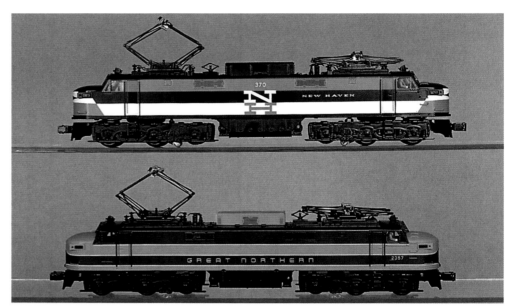

		MSRP	Current
20–2048	Canadian Pacific SD60M Diesel Locomotive Blue/Sliver; 1994		
	(–0) 3-Rail w/ Horn	279	350
	(–1) 3-Rail w/ Proto-Sound	349	425
	(–2) 2-Rail	279	350
SD70			
20–2154	Burlington Northern Santa Fe SD70MAC Diesel Locomotive numbered 9966 Green/White; 1997		
	(–1) 3-Rail w/ Proto-Sound	399	300
	(–2) 2-Rail	299	300
20–2155	Canadian National SD70MAC Diesel Locomotive Red/Black/White; 1997		
	(–1) 3-Rail w/ Proto-Sound	399	320
	(–2) 2-Rail	299	320

		MSRP	Current
SD80			
20–2190	Conrail SD80 Diesel Locomotive Blue/White; 1998		
	(–1) 3-Rail w/ Proto-Sound	330	375
SD90			
20–2184	Electro-Motive Division SD90MAC Demonstrator Diesel Locomotive numbered 8205 Blue/Teal/White; 1998		
	(–1) 3-Rail w/ Proto-Sound	330	400
20–2191	Union Pacific SD90MAC Diesel Locomotive numbered 8048, 8200, and 8223 Yellow; 1998		
	(–1) 3-Rail w/ Proto-Sound	330	400

		MSRP	Current
AEM7			
20–5505	Amtrak AEM7 Electric Locomotive Silver/Red/Blue/White; 1999		
	(−1) 3-Rail w/ Proto-Sound	330	CP
20–5506	SEPTA AEM7 Electric Locomotive Silver/Blue/Red; 1999		
	(−1) 3-Rail w/ Proto-Sound	330	CP
P-2 Box Cab			
20–5507	New York Central P-2 Box Cab Electric Locomotive Two-tone Gray; 1999		
	(−1) 3-Rail w/ Proto-Sound	600	CP
EP-5			
20–2195	New Haven EP-5 Electric Engine numbered 370 Black/Orange/White; 1999		
	(−1) 3-Rail w/ Proto-Sound	350	400
20–2196	Great Northern EP-5 Electric Engine numbered 2357 Green/Orange; 1999		
	(−1) 3-Rail w/ Proto-Sound	350	380

		MSRP	Current
20–2197	New Haven EP-5 Electric Engine Boxed Set Black/Orange/White; 1999		
	(−1)	550	600
GG-1			
20–5501	Pennsylvania RR GG-1 Electric Engine numbered 4876 Tuscan Red w/ 5 Gold stripes; 1997		
	(−1) 3-Rail w/ Proto-Sound	550	700
20–5502	Conrail GG-1 Electric Engine numbered 4800 Blue; 1997		
	(−1) 3-Rail w/ Proto-Sound	550	625
20–5503	Pennsylvania RR GG-1 Electric Engine numbered 4872 Silver w/ solid stripe; 1999		
	(−1) 3-Rail w/ Proto-Sound	600	600
20–5504	Pennsylvania RR GG-1 Electric Engine numbered 4935 Brunswick Green w/ 5 Gold stripes; 1999		
	(−1) 3-Rail w/ Proto-Sound	600	600

2 INCH HF COMP SHOES

Premier Line
Rolling Stock

Premier rolling stock is available in an impressive variety of types and road names. Equipped with Lionel-compatible knuckle couplers for toy train use, each car has been designed and manufactured as an accurate O scale model and carries accurate prototype decoration. All carbodies are made of ABS and feature die-cast trucks, brake wheels, fast-angle wheelsets, and needle-point axles. These big, rugged scale models look best when pulled by scale-proportioned three-rail loco-motives from MTH or other three-rail manufacturers.

Number 20-97400 4-Bay, 100-Ton Cylindrical Hopper Canada and 29-95007 Union Pacific Husky Stack Car

Premier Line 40′ Boxcars: left to right, top to bottom

20-9300 New York Central 159895,
20-9301 Union Pacific "The Challenger Merchandise Service" 9146
20-9302 Pennsylvania 24086, 20-9303 Santa Fe 31440
20-9304 Southern 550555, 20-9305 RailBox RBOX 15000
20-93006 Canadian National 481746,
20-93007 Illinois Central 12191
20-93008 Missouri Pacific 120112,
20-93009 Western Maryland 27209
20-93010 Missouri-Kansas-Texas (Katy) 97627, 20-93011 Container Corporation of America TLDX 20

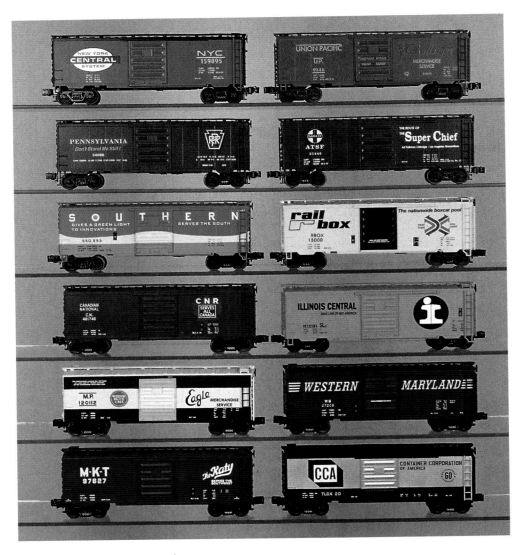

Boxcars, Refrigerator Cars, and Stock Cars

PS-1 40′ Boxcars

		MSRP	Current
20-9300	New York Central PS-1 40′ Boxcar numbered 159895 Jade Green; 1996	40	70
20-9301	Union Pacific PS-1 40′ Boxcar numbered 9146 Gray/Yellow lettered "The Challenger Merchandise Service"; 1996	40	110
20-9302	Pennsylvania RR PS-1 40′ Boxcar numbered 24086 Tuscan Red lettered "Don't Stand Me Still"; 1996	40	49
20-9303	Santa Fe PS-1 40′ Boxcar numbered 31440 Tuscan Red lettered "The Route of the Super Chief"; 1996	40	52
20-9304	Southern PS-1 40′ Boxcar numbered 550555 Blue/Yellow lettered "Gives a Green Light to Innovation/Serves the South"; 1997	40	45
20-9305	RailBox PS-1 40′ Boxcar numbered RBOX 15000 Yellow; 1997	40	37
20-93006	Canadian National PS-1 40′ Boxcar numbered 481746 Tuscan Red lettered "Serves All Canada"; 1997	40	39
20-93007	Illinois Central PS-1 40′ Boxcar numbered 12191 Orange lettered "Main Line of Mid-America"; 1997	40	39

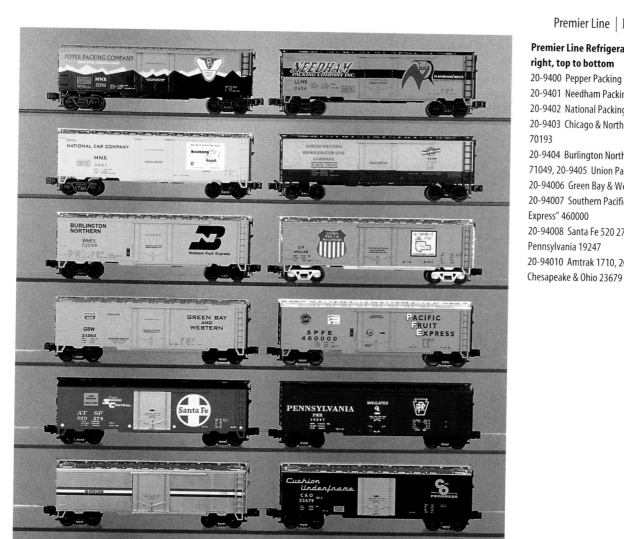

Premier Line Refrigerator Cars: left to right, top to bottom
20-9400 Pepper Packing Co. MNX 2319,
20-9401 Needham Packing Co. LLNX 2454
20-9402 National Packing Co. MNX 2421,
20-9403 Chicago & North Western NWX 70193
20-9404 Burlington Northern WHEX 71049, 20-9405 Union Pacific 490148
20-94006 Green Bay & Western 21002,
20-94007 Southern Pacific "Pacific Fruit Express" 460000
20-94008 Santa Fe 520 274, 20-94009 Pennsylvania 19247
20-94010 Amtrak 1710, 20-94011 Chesapeake & Ohio 23679

	MSRP	Current
20-93008 Missouri Pacific PS-1 40' Boxcar numbered 120112 Blue lettered "Eagle Merchandise Service"; 1998	40	42
20-93009 Western Maryland PS-1 40' Boxcar numbered 27209 Tuscan Red; 1998	40	34
20-93010 Missouri-Kansas-Texas PS-1 40' Boxcar numbered 97627 Tuscan Red lettered "The Katy Serves the Southwest"; 1998	40	40
20-93011 Container Corporation of America PS-1 40' Boxcar numbered TLDX 20 Silver/Black; 1998	40	43

	MSRP	Current
20-93014 Great Northern PS-1 40' Boxcar Lt. Green/White; 1999	40	CP
20-93015 New Haven PS-1 40' Boxcar numbered 22114 Tuscan Red; 1999	40	CP
20-93018 Bangor and Aroostook PS-1 40' Boxcar Red/White/Blue; 1999	40	CP
20-93019 Susquehanna PS-1 40' Boxcar Blue/Yellow; 1999	40	CP
20-93024 NYC PS-1 40' Boxcar numbered P&E 4503 Jade Green lettered "MTH Club 1999"; 1999	N/A	CP

**Premier Line Extended-Vision
Cabooses: left to right, top to bottom**
20-9100 Union Pacific 25214, 20-9101
Pennsylvania 477531
20-9102 Chesapeake & Ohio 3289, 20-9103
Norfolk & Western 562624
20-9104 Chessie System 903192, 20-9105
Santa Fe 999793
20-91008 Southern Pacific 324, 20-91009
Southern X252
20-91010 Santa Fe 999539, 20-91012
Conrail 22000
20-91013 Union Pacific 25461

	MSRP	Current
Double-Door 50′ Boxcars		
20-93012 Union Pacific Double-Door 50′ Boxcar		
Tuscan Red; 1998	43	45
20-93013 Louisville & Nashville Double-Door 50′ Boxcar		
Tuscan Red; 1998	43	45
20-93016 Pennsylvania RR Double-Door 50′ Boxcar		
Tuscan Red; 1999	43	CP
20-93017 Delaware & Hudson Double-Door 50′ Boxcar		
Tuscan Red; 1999	43	CP
20-93025 Ralston Purina 50′ Double-Door Plugged Boxcar		
Red; 1999	43	CP

	MSRP	Current
20-93026 Boston & Maine 50′ Double-Door Plugged Boxcar		
Blue; 1999	43	CP
50′ Boxcars		
20-93021 Union Pacific 50′ Boxcar		
Tuscan Red; 1999	43	CP
20-93022 Nickel Plate 50′ Boxcar		
Tuscan Red; 1999	43	CP
20-93027 Amtrak Mail 50′ Boxcar		
Silver; 1999	43	CP

Refrigerator Cars

		MSRP	Current
20-9400	Pepper Packing Reefer numbered MNX 2319 Blue lettered "Denver Colorado"; 1996	40	43
20-9401	Needham Packing Company, Inc. Reefer numbered LLNX 2454 Blue lettered "Flavorland Meats"; 1996	40	30
20-9402	National Packing Reefer numbered MNX 2421 Yellow lettered "National Car Company"; 1996	40	39
20-9403	Chicago & North Western Reefer numbered NWX 70193 Yellow/Green lettered "North Western Refrigerator Line"; 1996	40	99
20-9404	Burlington Northern Reefer numbered WHEX 71049 Yellow lettered "Western Fruit Express"; 1997	40	34
20-9405	Union Pacific Reefer numbered 490148 Yellow lettered "Automated Rail Way"; 1997	40	99
20-94006	Green Bay & Western Reefer numbered 21002 Yellow lettered "Green Bay Route"; 1997	40	36
20-94007	Southern Pacific Reefer numbered 460000 Orange lettered "Pacific Fruit Express"; 1997	40	35
20-94008	Santa Fe Reefer numbered 520 274 Red lettered "Super Shock Control"; 1998	40	37
20-94009	Pennsylvania RR Reefer numbered 19247 Tuscan Red; 1998	40	38
20-94010	Amtrak Reefer numbered 1710 Silver; 1998	40	50
20-94011	Chesapeake & Ohio Reefer numbered 23679 Blue lettered "Cushion Underframe"; 1998	40	40
20-94012	New Haven Reefer numbered 45097 Tuscan Red/White; 1999	40	CP
20-94013	Florida East Coast Reefer numbered 602 Red/White; 1999	40	CP

Stock Cars

		MSRP	Current
20-94501	Southern Steel-Sided Stock Car Brown; 1999	40	CP
20-94502	Union Pacific Steel-Sided Stock Car Yellow; 1999	40	CP
20-94503	Pennsylvania Steel-Sided Stock Car Tuscan Red; 1999	40	CP

Cabooses

Extended-Vision Cabooses

		MSRP	Current
20-9100	Union Pacific Extended-Vision Caboose numbered 25214 Yellow; 1996	45	90
20-9101	Pennsylvania RR Extended-Vision Caboose numbered 477531 Tuscan Red; 1996	45	65
20-9102	Chesapeake & Ohio Extended-Vision Caboose numbered 3289 Blue; 1996	45	60
20-9103	Norfolk & Western Extended-Vision Caboose numbered 562624 Red; 1996	45	65
20-9104	Chessie System Extended-Vision Caboose numbered 903192 Yellow; 1997	45	45
20-9105	Santa Fe Extended-Vision Caboose numbered 999793 Red; 1997	45	85
20-91006	Electro-Motive Division Extended-Vision Caboose numbered 5062 Blue/White; 1997	45	50
20-91007	Canadian National Extended-Vision Caboose numbered 79575 Red; 1997	45	50
20-91008	Southern Pacific Extended-Vision Caboose numbered 324 Brown/Orange; 1998	45	60
20-91009	Southern Extended-Vision Caboose numbered X252 Red; 1998	45	60
20-91010	Santa Fe Extended-Vision Caboose numbered 999539 Blue; 1998	45	60
20-91011	Chicago & North Western Extended-Vision Caboose Yellow; 1998	45	60

Premier Line Flatcars and Intermodal Cars: left to right, top to bottom
20-98101 West Virginia Pulp & Paper Co. w/logs 150, 20-98102 Western Maryland 2317
20-98104 Pennsylvania w/trailer 469677, 20-98105 Northern Pacific w/trailer 66152
20-98107 Union Pacific w/trailer 57256, 20-98108 Delaware & Hudson w/trailer 16144

		MSRP	Current
20-91012	Conrail Extended-Vision Caboose numbered 22000 Blue; 1998	45	65
20-91013	Union Pacific Extended-Vision Caboose numbered 25461 Yellow; 1998	45	70
20-91020	Lehigh Valley Extended-Vision Caboose Tuscan Red; 1999	45	CP
20-91021	New Haven Extended-Vision Caboose Orange; 1999	45	CP

N-8 Cabooses

20-91014	Pennsylvania RR N-8 Caboose Tuscan Red/Black; 1999	45	CP

Steel Cabooses

20-91015	Duluth, Missabe & Iron Range Steel Caboose Yellow; 1999	45	CP
20-91016	Great Northern Steel Caboose Blue/White; 1999	45	CP
20-91017	Norfolk & Western Steel Caboose Red/White; 1999	45	CP

		MSRP	Current
20-91018	Santa Fe Steel Caboose Red/Yellow; 1999	45	CP

Flatcars and Intermodal Cars

Flatcars

20-98101	West Virginia Pulp & Paper Co. Flatcar numbered 150; includes log load Black; 1997	43	44
20-98102	Western Maryland Flatcar numbered 2317; includes log load Gray; 1997	43	47
20-98103	West Virginia Pulp & Paper Co. 3-Car Flatcar Set Black; 1997	120	160
20-98104	Pennsylvania RR Flatcar numbered 469677; includes two Pennsylvania RR "TrucTrain" trailers Tuscan Red; 1998	45	45
20-98105	Northern Pacific Flatcar numbered 66152; includes two "Northern Pacific" trailers Black; 1998	45	45
20-98107	Union Pacific Flatcar numbered 57256; includes two Union Pacific "PEOPLE…on the move" trailers Brown lettered "Road of the Streamliners"; 1999	45	CP

Premier Line Intermodal Well Cars and Spine Car Sets: top to bottom
20-9502 Burlington Northern Husky Stack Well Car 60000
20-95004 Hanjin Husky Stack Well Car DTTX 56148
20-95006 Maersk Husky Stack Well Car MAEX100052
20-95035 TTAX Spine Car (5-Car Set)
20-95036 Conrail Spine Car (5-Car Set)

		MSRP	Current
20-98108	Delaware & Hudson Flatcar numbered 16144; includes two "Delaware & Hudson" trailers Red; 1999	45	CP
20-98110	Baltimore & Ohio Flatcar; includes two Baltimore & Ohio "TOFCEE Service" trailers Blue; 1999	45	CP
20-98111	Santa Fe Flatcar; includes two Santa Fe "Piggy-Back Service" trailers Brown; 1999	45	CP

Depressed-Center Flatcars

		MSRP	Current
20-98106	Union Pacific 75′ Depressed-Center Flatcar Yellow; 1998	50	50
20-98109	Nickel Plate Road 75′ Depressed-Center Flatcar Blue; 1999	50	CP

Center-Beam Flatcars

		MSRP	Current
20-98211	CSX Center-Beam Flatcar Black; 1998	45	50
20-98212	Union Pacific Center-Beam Flatcar Tuscan Red; 1998	45	50

Premier Line Gondolas: left to right, top to bottom
20-98001 Pennsylvania (w/o load) 385405, 20-98002 Union Pacific (w/o load) 30294
20-98003 Southern Pacific 339288, 20-98004 Southern 60750
20-98005 Chicago & North Western 340511, 20-98006 Seaboard Coast Line 6950
20-98007 Delaware & Hudson 15468, 20-98008 Lehigh Valley 34679

		MSRP	Current
20-98229	CP Rail Center-Beam Flatcar Red; 1999	45	CP
20-98230	Tobacco Valley Lumber Center-Beam Flatcar Lt. Blue; 1999	45	CP

Automobile Carrier
20-98231	Denver Rio Grande Corrugated Auto Carrier Orange; 1999	45	CP

Intermodal Well Cars
20-9501	TTUX Husky Stack Well Car Yellow; 1996	50	60
20-9502	Burlington Northern Husky Stack Well Car numbered 60000; includes two white containers (BNAU 780253) Red; 1996	50	60
20-95003	Southern Pacific Husky Stack Well Car numbered GBRX 2415 Red; 1997	50	50
20-95004	Hanjin Husky Stack Well Car numbered DTTX 56148; includes two blue containers (HJCU 747 429 9) Yellow; 1997	50	50
20-95005	Burlington Northern Santa Fe Husky Stack Well Car White/Orange; 1998	50	55

		MSRP	Current
20-95006	Maersk Husky Stack Well Car numbered MAEX100052; includes two white containers (MAEX 516 243 9 and MAEX 516 244 9) Light Blue; 1998	50	55
20-95006	Burlington Northern Santa Fe Husky Stack Well Car (See Set 20-2172) White/Orange; 1998	N/A	N/A
20-95007	Union Pacific Husky Stack Well Car White/Yellow; 1998	50	50
20-95007	Burlington Northern Santa Fe Husky Well Stack Car (See Set 20-2172) White/Orange; 1998	N/A	N/A
20-95011	Burlington Northern Santa Fe Husky Well Stack Set w/ End-of-Train Device Orange/White; 1998	N/A	70

Intermodal Spine Cars
20-95035	TTAX 5-Car Spine Car Set; includes various containers and trailers Yellow; 1997	200	205
20-95036	Conrail 5-Car Spine Car Set; includes various containers and trailers Yellow; 1998	200	205

Gondolas and Coil Cars

Scale Length Gondolas
20-98001	Pennsylvania RR Gondola numbered 385405 Black; 1997	37	35

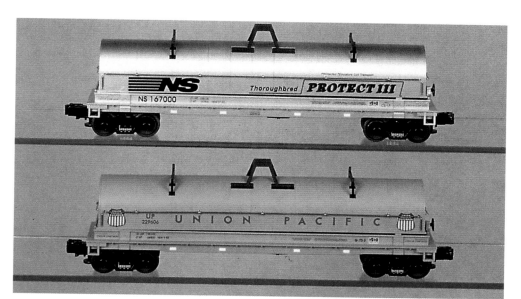

Left: Premier Line Coil Cars: top to bottom
20-98203 Norfolk Southern 167000
20-98204 Union Pacific 229606

Below: Premier Line 4-Bay Hopper and Coalporter Hopper Cars: left to right, top to bottom
20-97402 Western Maryland 90000 (4-bay hoppers), 20-97403 Union Pacific 37216
20-97407 CSX 346894, 20-97408 Norfolk & Western 131410
20-9700 CSX 390598 (Coalporters),
20-9701 Burlington Northern 534204
20-97003 Detroit Edison 6105

	MSRP	Current			MSRP	Current
20-98002 Union Pacific Gondola numbered 30294 Tuscan Red; 1997	37	32	**20-98004** Southern Gondola numbered 60750; includes junk load Tuscan Red; 1998		37	35
20-98003 Southern Pacific Gondola numbered 339288; includes junk load Tuscan Red; 1998	37	38	**20-98005** Chicago & North Western Gondola numbered 340511 includes junk load Green; 1998		37	35

Premier Line Wood Chip Hopper Cars
20-97501 Southern 13975
20-97502 Northern Pacific 119743

		MSRP	Current
20-98006	Seaboard Coast Line Gondola numbered 6950; includes junk load Tuscan Red; 1998	37	35
20-98007	Delaware & Hudson Gondola numbered 15468; includes junk load Black; 1999	37	CP
20-98008	Lehigh Valley Gondola numbered 34679; includes junk load Jade Green; 1999	37	CP

Coil Cars

		MSRP	Current
20-98203	Norfolk Southern Coil Car numbered 167000 Silver lettered "Thoroughbred Protect III"; 1998	40	45
20-98204	Union Pacific Coil Car numbered 229606 Yellow; 1998	40	45
20-98213	New Haven Coil Car numbered 62004 Orange/Black/White; 1999	40	CP
20-98214	Southern Pacific Coil Car numbered 595632 Gray/Red/White; 1999	40	CP

Hopper Cars

Ore Cars

		MSRP	Current
20-97505	Duluth, Missabe & Iron Range 6-Car Ore Car Set Tuscan Red; 1999	180	CP
20-97506	Duluth, Missabe & Iron Range 6-Car Ore Car Set Tuscan Red; 1999	180	CP

2-Bay Offset Hopper Cars

		MSRP	Current
20-97415	Frisco 2-Bay Offset Hopper Car Red/Black; 1999	40	CP
20-97416	Chesapeake & Ohio 2-Bay Offset Hopper Car Black/White; 1999	40	CP

4-Bay Hopper Cars

		MSRP	Current
20-97057	Norfolk & Western 4-Bay Hopper 6-Car Set Black/White; 1999	230	CP
20-97058	Santa Fe 4-Bay Hopper 6-Car Set Tuscan Red/White; 1999	230	CP
20-97059	Union Pacific 4-Bay Hopper 6-Car Set; includes six individually numbered 4-bay hopper cars Tuscan Red; 1999	230	CP
20-97060	Union Pacific 4-Bay Hopper 6-Car Set; includes six individually numbered 4-bay hopper cars Tuscan Red; 1999	230	CP
20-97402	Western Maryland 4-Bay Hopper Car numbered 90000 Gray; 1998	40	35
20-97403	Union Pacific 4-Bay Hopper Car numbered 37216 Tuscan Red; 1998	40	40
20-97404	Union Pacific 4-Bay Hopper 6-Car Set Tuscan Red; 1998	230	230
20-97407	CSX 4-Bay Hopper Car numbered 346894 Black; 1998	40	40
20-97408	Norfolk & Western 4-Bay Hopper Car numbered 131410 Black; 1998	40	45

	MSRP	Current

Coalporter Hopper Cars

20-9700 CSX Coalporter Hopper Car numbered 390598
Black; 1997 — **43** — **50**

20-9701 Burlington Northern Coalporter Hopper Car numbered 534204
Silver; 1997 — **43** — **50**

20-97002 Burlington Northern Santa Fe Coalporter Hopper Car
Silver/Green; 1997 — **43** — **43**

Premier Line PS-2 Covered Hopper Cars: left to right, top to bottom
20-97101 Union Pacific 19395, 20-97102 Chessie System B&O 631123
20-97103 Rock Island 500700, 20-97104 Illinois Central Gulf 700311
20-97105 Burlington CB&Q 189312, 20-97106 Pennsylvania 257128
20-97107 Atlantic Coast Line 89134, 20-97108 New York Central 87615
20-97109 Milwaukee Road 52495

	MSRP	Current

20-97003 Detroit Edison Coalporter Hopper Car numbered 6105
Gray; 1997 — **43** — **44**

Premier 3-Bay Cylindrical Hopper Cars
20-97405 Chessie System B&O 101476
20-97406 Santa Fe 314952

Premier Line 4-Bay, 100-Ton Cylindrical Hopper Cars
20-97400 Canada CNWX 110060
20-97401 North American NAHX 455002

		MSRP	Current
Rapid Discharge Hopper Cars			
20-98217	Florida East Coast Rapid Discharge Car Red/Yellow; 1999	43	CP
20-98218	Atlantic Coast Line Rapid Discharge Car Silver/Orange; 1999	43	CP
Wood Chip Hopper Cars			
20-97501	Southern Wood Chip Hopper Car numbered 13975 Tuscan Red; 1998	40	35
20-97502	Northern Pacific Wood Chip Hopper Car numbered 119743 Tuscan Red; 1998	40	35

		MSRP	Current
20-97503	Santa Fe Wood Chip Hopper Car numbered 16573 Brown; 1999	40	CP
20-97504	Southern Pacific Wood Chip Hopper Car Tuscan Red; 1999	40	CP
PS-2 Covered Hopper Cars			
20-97101	Union Pacific PS-2 Hopper Car numbered 19395 Gray; 1997	40	36
20-97102	Chessie PS-2 Hopper Car numbered B&O 631123 Yellow; 1997	40	36
20-97103	Rock Island PS-2 Hopper Car numbered 500700 Lt. Blue lettered "The Rock"; 1997	40	36

	MSRP	Current
20-97104 Illinois Central Gulf PS-2 Hopper Car numbered 700311 Gray; 1997	40	36
20-97105 Burlington PS-2 Hopper Car numbered CB&Q 189312 Red; 1997	40	38
20-97106 Pennsylvania RR PS-2 Hopper Car numbered 257128 Gray; 1997	40	36
20-97107 Atlantic Coast Line PS-2 Hopper Car numbered 89134 Yellow; 1998	40	40
20-97108 New York Central PS-2 Hopper Car numbered 87615 Jade Green; 1998	40	41

Premier Line 8,000-Gallon Tank Cars: left to right, top to bottom
20-9600 Norfolk Southern 67845, 20-9601 Conrail 2315
20-96002 Vulcan Chemicals VMCX 1203, 20-96003 CSX 67826
20-96004 National Starch and Chemical UTLX 76910, 20-96005 Ethyl Corporation EBAX 6039
20-96015 Geigy Chemical Corporation 88383

	MSRP	Current
20-97109 Milwaukee Road PS-2 Hopper Car numbered 52495 Orange; 1999	40	CP
20-97110 Nickel Plate PS-2 Hopper Car numbered 99920 Black/White; 1999	40	CP
20-97111 Great Northern PS-2 Hopper Car numbered 71436 Gray; 1999	40	CP

Premier Line Unibody Tank Cars: left to right, top to bottom
20-9200 Burlington Northern 12688, 20-9201 Denver & Rio Grande 10009
20-9202 New York Central "Pacemaker" 1750, 20-9203 Chicago & North Western 3478
20-9204 Pennsylvania 6789, 20-9205 Union Pacific 67890
20-92006 Southern Pacific 34890, 20-92007 Chessie System 8209

3-Bay Cylindrical Hopper Cars

		MSRP	Current
20-97405	Chessie 3-Bay Cylindrical Hopper Car numbered B&O 101476 Yellow; 1998	43	40
20-97406	Santa Fe 3-Bay Cylindrical Hopper Car numbered 314952 Tuscan Red; 1998	43	40
20-97417	Union Pacific 3-Bay Cylindrical Hopper Car Gray; 1999	43	CP
20-97418	Canada 3-Bay Cylindrical Hopper Car Red; 1999	43	CP

100-Ton Cylindrical Hopper Cars

		MSRP	Current
20-97400	Canada 100-Ton Cylindrical Hopper Car numbered CNWX 110060 Red; 1997	45	50
20-97401	North American 100-Ton Cylindrical Hopper Car numbered NAHX 455002 Silver; 1997	45	50
20-97409	Lehigh Valley 100-Ton Cylindrical Hopper Car numbered 50339 Maroon/White; 1999	45	CP
20-97410	Burlington 100-Ton Cylindrical Hopper Car numbered FW&D 3223 Gray/Red; 1999	45	CP

Tank Cars

8,000-Gallon Tank Cars

		MSRP	Current
20-9600	Norfolk Southern 8,000-Gallon Tank Car numbered 67845 Black; 1997	40	37

		MSRP	Current
20-9601	Conrail 8,000-Gallon Tank Car numbered 2315 Blue; 1997	**40**	**40**
20-96002	Vulcan Chemicals 8,000-Gallon Tank Car numbered VMCX 1203 Gray/Yellow; 1997	**40**	**36**
20-96003	CSX 8,000-Gallon Tank Car numbered 67826 Gray; 1997	**40**	**36**
20-96004	National Starch and Chemical 8,000-Gallon Tank Car numbered UTLX 76910 White; 1998	**40**	**45**
20-96005	Ethyl Corporation 8,000-Gallon Tank Car numbered EBAX 6039 Gray lettered "antiknock compound"; 1998	**40**	**40**
20-96014	Kodak 8,000-Gallon Tank Car Yellow; 1999	**40**	**NM**
20-96015	Geigy Chemical Corporation 8,000-Gallon Tank Car numbered 88383 White/Black; 1999	**40**	**CP**

Premier Line Unibody Tank Cars: left to right, top to bottom
20-92008 GATX Tank Train 44587, 20-92009 Southern 995006
20-96008 Hooker Chemical SHPX 5867, 20-96009 Seaboard System 67890
20-92010 Burlington Northern Santa Fe 12687, 20-92011 Airco Industrial Gases ARIX 3008

		MSRP	Current
20-96018	Klasen Oil Company 8,000-Gallon Tank Car numbered CB 16142 Orange/Black lettered "Big Mo"; 1999 (uncataloged, H. Turner)	**42**	**CP**

Unibody Tank Cars

		MSRP	Current
20-9200	Burlington Northern Unibody Tank Car numbered 12688 Black/Green; 1996	**43**	**100**
20-9201	Denver & Rio Grande Western Unibody Tank Car numbered 10009 Orange/Silver lettered "The Action Road"; 1996	**43**	**100**
20-9202	New York Central Unibody Tank Car numbered 1750 Gray/Red lettered "Pacemaker Freight Service"; 1996	**43**	**80**
20-9203	Chicago & North Western Unibody Tank Car numbered 3478 Green/Yellow lettered "Falcon Service"; 1996	**43**	**90**

Premier Line Hot Metal Cars
20-98201 Black 52
20-98210 Pennsylvania 5

		MSRP	Current
20-9204	Pennsylvania RR Unibody Tank Car numbered 6789 Black; 1997	43	90
20-9205	Union Pacific Unibody Tank Car numbered 67890 Yellow/Gray; 1997	43	85
20-92006	Southern Pacific Unibody Tank Car numbered 34890 Black/Orange; 1997	43	49
20-92007	Chessie System Unibody Tank Car numbered 8209 Yellow/Black; 1997	43	45
20-92008	GATX Unibody Tank Car numbered 44587 Black lettered "TankTrain"; 1998	43	39
20-92009	Southern Unibody Tank Car numbered 995006 Black; 1998	43	39
20-92010	Burlington Northern Santa Fe Unibody Tank Car numbered 12687 Green/Orange; 1998	43	50
20-92011	Airco Industrial Gases Unibody Tank Car numbered ARIX 3008 Orange/White lettered "Liquid Nitrogen Only"; 1998	43	45
20-96008	Hooker Chemical Unibody Tank Car numbered SHPX 5867 Orange; 1998	43	45
20-96009	Seaboard System Unibody Tank Car numbered 67890 Gray; 1998	43	45

		MSRP	Current
20-96016	Santa Fe Unibody Tank Car numbered ATSF 142473 Black/Red/Yellow; 1999	43	CP
20-96017	Great Northern Oil Unibody Tank Car marked UTLX 76488 Yellow/Black; 1999	43	CP

20,000-Gallon 4-Compartment Tank Cars

		MSRP	Current
20-96010	Burlington Northern 20,000-Gallon 4-Compartment Tank Car Green/Orange; 1999	45	CP
20-96011	ETCX 20,000-Gallon 4-Compartment Tank Car Gray/Black; 1999	45	CP

33,000-Gallon Tank Cars

		MSRP	Current
20-96006	Suburban Propane 33,000-Gallon Tank Car Cream; 1998	45	45
20-96007	Pyrofax Gas 33,000-Gallon Tank Car White; 1998	45	45
20-96012	Royster 33,000-Gallon Tank Car Gray/Red; 1999	45	CP
20-96013	Union Texas Petroleum 33,000-Gallon Tank Car Gray/Red; 1999	45	CP

Hot Metal Cars

		MSRP	Current
20-98201	Hot Metal Car numbered 52 Black; 1997	50	60
20-98202	Hot Metal Car Silver; 1997	50	70

		MSRP	Current
20-98209	CSX Hot Metal Car numbered 2 Black; 1998	50	50
20-98210	Pennsylvania RR Hot Metal Car numbered 5 Silver; 1998	50	50

Work Cars

Scale Test Cars

		MSRP	Current
20-98215	Union Pacific Die-Cast Test Car; O scale Silver; 1999	50	CP
20-98216	Pennsylvania RR Die-Cast Test Car; O scale Black; 1999	50	CP

Crane Cars

		MSRP	Current
20-98221	Lehigh Valley Crane Car; O scale N/A; 1999	70	CP
20-98222	Great Northern Crane Car; O scale Orange/Black; 1999	70	CP

Crane Tenders

		MSRP	Current
20-98223	Lehigh Valley Crane Tender; scale length N/A; 1999	43	CP
20-98224	Great Northern Crane Tender; scale length N/A; 1999	43	CP

Jordan Spreaders

		MSRP	Current
20-98205	Union Pacific Jordan Spreader Yellow; 1998	70	70
20-98206	Pennsylvania RR Jordan Spreader Black; 1998	70	70
20-98225	Baltimore & Ohio Jordan Spreader Black; 1999	70	CP
20-98226	Denver & Rio Grande Jordan Spreader Yellow; 1999	70	CP

Snow Plows

		MSRP	Current
20-98207	Union Pacific Snow Plow Gray; 1998	60	65
20-98208	Pennsylvania RR Snow Plow Yellow; 1998	60	65
20-98219	New York Central Snow Plow Brown; 1999	60	CP
20-98220	Conrail Snow Plow Black; 1999	60	CP
20-98227	Chicago & North Western Snow Plow Yellow; 1999	60	CP
20-98228	Canadian National Snow Plow Red; 1999	60	CP

Mixed Sets

		MSRP	Current
20-90001	Reading 6-Car Freight Set Various; 1999	230	CP
20-90002	Nickel Plate 6-Car Freight Set Various; 1999	230	CP
20-90003	Pennsylvania RR 6-Car Freight Set Various; 1999	230	CP
20-90004	MTH 4-Car Freight Set Various; 1999	230	CP
20-90005	Pennsylvania 6-Car Freight Set; includes Madison coach, 4-bay hopper, flatcar w/ freight trucks, crane, gondola w/ junk load, N-8 caboose N/A; 1999	230	CP
20-90006	Great Northern 6-Car Freight Set; includes 50' boxcar, stock car, 3-bay cylindrical hopper, tank car, flatcar w/20' trailers, steel caboose N/A; 1999	230	CP
20-90007	Burlington Northern Merger Series Freight Set; includes Spokane, Portland & Seattle log car, Burlington Route reefer car, Northern Pacific boxcar N/A; 1999	100	CP

Premier Line
Passenger Cars

P remier passenger cars in the MTH line complement both their steam and diesel locomotives in road-names, paint schemes, and body types (heavyweight or streamlined in different lengths) and configurations (baggage, coach, diner, etc.). Offered as four- or five-car sets with add-on cars following later, the colorful passenger cars come in a variety of body types and lengths, ride on die-cast trucks, have operating knuckle couplers and illuminated interiors, and are smooth-sided or ribbed, plated or painted. Scale fidelity is not evident in the Premier passenger line as in steam engines, diesel locomotives, and freight cars; nevertheless, the cars look handsome and are worthy of the "Premier" category.

Aluminum Observation Car 3198 from the 20-2153 (30-2153 on box) Santa Fe *El Capitan* Set

Premier Line 70', Madison-Style Santa Fe 5-Car Passenger Set: top to bottom

20-4007 Santa Fe baggage 1812
             Santa Fe coach 3000
             Santa Fe coach 3001
             Santa Fe coach 3002
             Santa Fe parlor/observation 3221

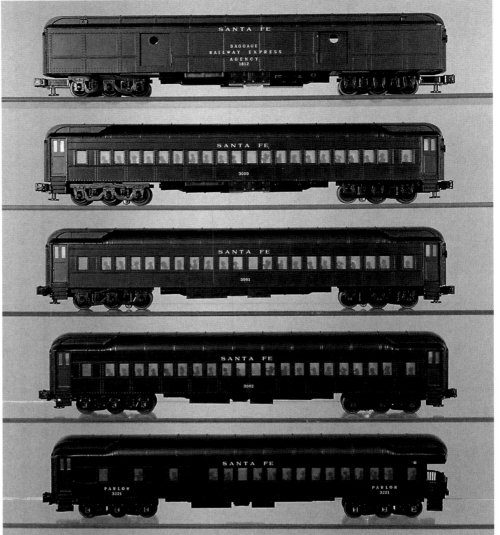

70' Madison

5-Car Sets

		MSRP	Current
20-4001	Baltimore & Ohio 5-Car 70' Madison Passenger Set Blue/Gray; 1995	299	430
20-4002	Delaware & Hudson 5-Car 70' Madison Passenger Set Blue/Gray; 1995	299	400
20-4003	Denver & Rio Grande Western 5-Car 70' Madison Passenger Set Yellow/Silver; 1995	299	495
20-4004	Norfolk & Western 5-Car 70' Madison Passenger Set Maroon/Black; 1995	299	400
20-4005	New York Central 5-Car 70' Madison Passenger Set Green; 1995	299	400
20-4006	Pennsylvania RR 5-Car 70' Madison Passenger Set Tuscan Red; 1995	299	425
20-4007	Santa Fe 5-Car 70' Madison Passenger Set; includes Railway Express Agency car no. 1812, coach 3000, coach 3001, coach 3002, and observation/parlor 3221 Green; 1995	299	500
20-4008	Southern 5-Car 70' Madison Passenger Set Green/Black; 1995	299	500
20-4009	Texas & Pacific 5-Car 70' Madison Passenger Set Blue/White; 1995	299	450

		MSRP	Current
20-4010	Lehigh Valley 5-Car 70' Madison Passenger Set Black/Red; 1995	299	450
20-4011	Union Pacific 5-Car 70' Madison Passenger Set Two-tone Gray; 1995	299	400
20-4012	Central RR of New Jersey 5-Car 70' Madison Passenger Set Green; 1995	300	300
20-4013	Chesapeake & Ohio 5-Car 70' Madison Passenger Set Blue/Gray; 1995	299	395
20-4014	Northern Pacific 5-Car 70' Madison Passenger Set Green/White; 1995	299	450
20-4015	Milwaukee Road 5-Car 70' Madison Passenger Set Orange/Black/Red; 1995	299	495
20-4016	Frisco 5-Car 70' Madison Passenger Set Red/White; 1995	299	475
20-4018	Pennsylvania RR 5-Car 70' Madison Passenger Set Tuscan Red; 1996	299	325
20-4019	New York Central 5-Car 70' Madison Passenger Set Green; 1996	299	325
20-4020	Pullman 5-Car 70' Madison Passenger Set Green; 1996	299	325
20-4021	Central RR of New Jersey 5-Car 70' Madison Passenger Set Blue; 1998	250	300
20-4022	New York Central 5-Car 70' Madison Passenger Set Green; 1998	250	250
20-4023	Pennsylvania RR 5-Car 70' Madison Passenger Set Tuscan Red; 1998	250	250
20-4024	Norfolk & Western 5-Car 70' Madison Passenger Set Tuscan Red; 1998	250	250
20-4025	Pennsylvania RR 5-Car 70' Madison Passenger Set Tuscan Red; 1999	250	CP
20-4026	New York Central 5-Car 70' Madison Passenger Set Two-tone Gray; 1999	250	CP
20-4027	Boston & Maine 5-Car 70' Madison Passenger Set Brown; 1999	250	CP

		MSRP	Current
20-4028	Chesapeake & Ohio 5-Car 70' Madison Passenger Set Blue/Yellow; 1999	250	CP

2-Car Sets

		MSRP	Current
20-4101	Baltimore & Ohio 2-Car 70' Madison Combine/Diner Passenger Set Blue/Gray; 1995	149	165
20-4103	Denver & Rio Grande Western 2-Car Madison Combine/Diner Passenger Set Silver/Yellow; 1994	N/A	160
20-4105	New York Central 2-Car 70' Madison Combine/Diner Passenger Set Green; 1995	149	180
20-4106	Pennsylvania RR 2-Car 70' Madison Combine/Diner Passenger Set Tuscan Red/Black; 1995	149	250
20-4107	Santa Fe 2-Car 70' Madison Combine/Diner Passenger Set Green; 1995	149	210
20-4108	Southern 2-Car 70' Madison Combine/Diner Passenger Set Green/Black; 1995	149	175
20-4109	Texas & Pacific 2-Car 70' Madison Combine/Diner Passenger Set Blue/White; 1995	149	175
20-4110	Lehigh Valley 2-Car 70' Madison Combine/Diner Passenger Set Black/Red; 1995	149	180
20-4111	Union Pacific 2-Car Madison Combine/Diner Passenger Set Two-tone Gray; 1994	149	200
20-4114	Northern Pacific 2-Car 70' Madison Combine/Diner Passenger Set Green/White; 1997	149	175
20-4118	Pennsylvania RR 2-Car 70' Madison Combine/Diner Passenger Set Tuscan Red; 1997	149	165
20-4119	New York Central 2-Car 70' Madison Combine/Diner Passenger Set Green; 1997	149	145
20-4120	Pullman 2-Car 70' Madison Combine/Diner Passenger Set Green; 1997	149	150

**Premier Line Santa Fe *El Capitan* 60′
4-Car Streamlined Passenger Set: top
to bottom**

20-2153 (30-2153 on box)
      Railway Express Agency 3430
      Coach 3103
      Vista Dome 500
      Observation 3198

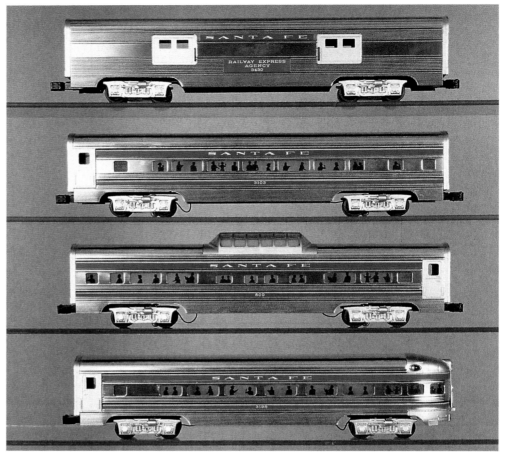

		MSRP	Current
20-4121	Central RR of New Jersey 2-Car 70′ Madison Combine/Diner Passenger Set Blue; 1999	**100**	**CP**
20-4122	New York Central 2-Car 70′ Madison Combine/Diner Passenger Set Green; 1999	**100**	**CP**
20-4124	Norfolk & Western 2-Car 70′ Madison Combine/Diner Passenger Set Red; 1999	**100**	**CP**
20-4125	Pennsylvania RR 2-Car 70′ Madison Combine/Diner Passenger Set Tuscan Red; 1999	**100**	**CP**
20-4126	New York Central 2-Car 70′ Madison Combine/Diner Passenger Set Two-tone Gray; 1999	**100**	**CP**
20-4127	Boston & Maine 2-Car 70′ Madison Combine/Diner Passenger Set Brown; 1999	**100**	**CP**

		MSRP	Current
20-4801	Baltimore & Ohio 2-Car Scale Madison Passenger Set N/A; 1994	**300**	**300**

60′ Streamlined

5-Car Sets

		MSRP	Current
20-6001	Union Pacific 5-Car 60′ Aluminum Passenger Set Smooth-sided; Yellow/Gray; 1995	**375**	**475**
20-6002	Denver & Rio Grande Western 5-Car 60′ Aluminum Passenger Set Smooth-sided; Silver/Yellow; 1995	**375**	**500**
20-6003	Pennsylvania RR 5-Car 60′ Aluminum Passenger Set Smooth-sided; Tuscan Red/Black; 1995	**375**	**425**
20-6004	Burlington 5-Car 60′ Aluminum Passenger Set Fluted ridges; Aluminum; 1995	**375**	**575**
20-6005	Florida East Coast 5-Car 60′ Aluminum Passenger Set Smooth-sided; Red/Gold; 1995	**375**	**600**

**Premier Line Louisville & Nashville 60'
4-Car Streamlined Passenger Set: top
to bottom**
20-6020 Baggage 1450
         Coach 3209
         Vista Dome "Mt. Norris"
         Observation "Royal Canal"

		MSRP	Current
20-6006	Delaware & Hudson 5-Car 60' Aluminum Passenger Set Smooth-sided; Silver/Blue; 1995	375	425
20-6007	Pennsylvania RR 5-Car 60' Aluminum Passenger Set Fluted ridges; Silver/Maroon; 1995	375	450
20-6008	Baltimore & Ohio 5-Car 60' Aluminum Passenger Set Smooth-sided; Blue/Gray; 1995	375	450
20-6009	Santa Fe 5-Car 60' Aluminum Passenger Set Smooth-sided; Aluminum; 1995	375	475
20-6010	New York Central 5-Car 60' Aluminum Passenger Set Smooth-sided; Gray/Black; 1995	375	475
20-6011	Canadian Pacific 5-Car 60' Aluminum Passenger Set Fluted ridges; Aluminum/Maroon; 1995	375	525
20-6012	Baltimore & Ohio 5-Car 60' Aluminum Passenger Set Smooth-sided; Blue/Gray/Yellow *Cincinnatian* scheme; 1995	375	500

4-Car Sets

		MSRP	Current
20-2153	Santa Fe *El Capitan* (4-Car 60' Aluminum Passenger) Boxed Set; includes F3 ABA diesel locomotives, Railway Express Agency car no. 3430, coach 3103, dome 500, and observation 3198 Fluted ridges; Silver/Red; 1997	939	1,200
20-6013	New York Central 4-Car 60' Aluminum Passenger Set Fluted ridges; Aluminum; 1996	299	400
20-6014	Norfolk & Western 4-Car 60' Aluminum Passenger Set Fluted ridges; Maroon/Black; 1996	299	550
20-6015	Union Pacific 4-Car 60' Aluminum Passenger Set Fluted ridges; Aluminum; 1996	299	425
20-6016	Santa Fe 4-Car 60' Aluminum Passenger Set Fluted ridges; Aluminum; 1996	299	470
20-6017	Pennsylvania RR 4-Car 60' Aluminum Passenger Set Tuscan Red; 1996	299	385

2-Car Sleeper/Diner Streamlined Passenger Set
20-6120 Sleeper "Alabama Pine"
   Diner "Dixie Journey"

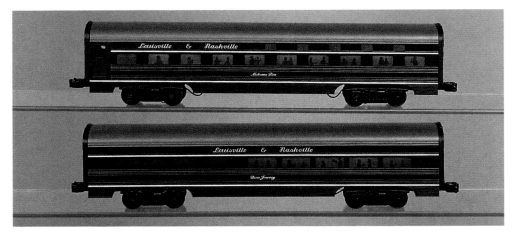

Premier Line Santa Fe *El Capitan* 60′ 2-Car Sleeper/Diner Streamlined Passenger Set
20-6122 (30-6122 on box)
   Diner 1505
   Sleeper "Laguna"

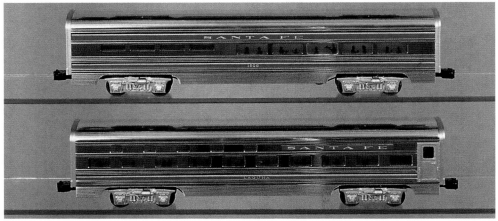

		MSRP	Current
20-6018	Santa Fe 4-Car 60′ Aluminum Passenger Set Smooth-sided; two-tone Blue "Blue Goose" scheme; 1996	**299**	**385**
20-6019	Union Pacific 4-Car 60′ Aluminum Passenger Set Smooth-sided; Yellow; 1996	**299**	**385**
20-6020	Louisville & Nashville 4-Car 60′ Aluminum Passenger Set; includes Railway Express Agency car no. 1450, coach 3209, dome "Mt. Norris," and observation "Royal Canal" Fluted ridges; Blue/Gray; 1997	**299**	**385**
20-6021	Santa Fe 4-Car 60′ Aluminum Passenger Set Fluted ridges; Silver/Red; 1997	**299**	**385**

2-Car Sets

		MSRP	Current
20-6102	Denver & Rio Grande Western 2-Car 60′ Sleeper/Diner Aluminum Passenger Set Smooth-sided; Silver/Yellow; 1996	**160**	**160**
20-6104	Burlington 2-Car 60′ Sleeper/Diner Aluminum Passenger Set Fluted ridges; Aluminum; 1996	**160**	**160**

		MSRP	Current
20-6105	Florida East Coast 2-Car 60′ Sleeper/Diner Aluminum Passenger Set Smooth-sided; Red/Gold; 1996	**160**	**160**
20-6108	Baltimore & Ohio 2-Car 60′ Sleeper/Diner Aluminum Passenger Set Smooth-sided; Blue/Gray; 1996	**160**	**16**0
20-6112	Baltimore & Ohio 2-Car 60′ Sleeper/Diner Aluminum Passenger Set Smooth-sided; Blue/Gray/Yellow *Cincinnatian* scheme; 1996	**160**	**160**
20-6113	New York Central 2-Car 60′ Sleeper/Diner Aluminum Passenger Set Fluted ridges; Aluminum; 1996	**160**	**160**
20-6114	Norfolk & Western 2-Car 60′ Sleeper/Diner Aluminum Passenger Set Fluted ridges; Maroon/Black; 1996	**160**	**160**
20-6116	Santa Fe 2-Car 60′ Sleeper/Diner Aluminum Passenger Set Fluted ridges; Aluminum; 1996	**160**	**160**

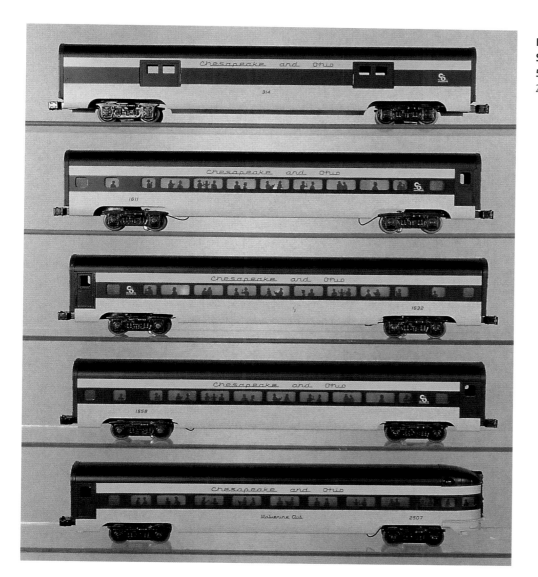

Premier Line Chesapeake & Ohio 70′ Smooth-Sided, Painted, Streamlined 5-Car Passenger Set: top to bottom
20-6502 baggage 314
coach 1611
coach 1632
coach 1658
observation 2507

		MSRP	Current
20-6117	Pennsylvania RR 2-Car 60′ Sleeper/Diner Aluminum Passenger Set Fluted ridges; Tuscan Red; 1996	**160**	**160**
20-6118	Santa Fe 2-Car 60′ Sleeper/Diner Aluminum Passenger Set Smooth-sided; two-tone Blue "Blue Goose" scheme; 1996	**160**	**160**
20-6119	Union Pacific 2-Car 60′ Sleeper/Diner Aluminum Passenger Set Smooth-sided; Yellow; 1996	**160**	**160**
20-6120	Louisville & Nashville 2-Car 60′ Sleeper/Diner Aluminum Passenger Set; includes sleeper "Alabama Pine" and diner "Dixie Journey" Fluted ridges; Blue/Gray; 1997	**160**	**160**

		MSRP	Current
20-6121	Santa Fe 2-Car 60′ Sleeper/Diner Aluminum Passenger Set Silver Regular Santa Fe Livery; 1997	**159**	**180**
20-6122	Santa Fe 2-Car 60′ Sleeper/Diner Aluminum Passenger Set (box numbered 30-6122); includes diner car no. 1505 and sleeper "Laguna" Fluted ridges; Silver/Red/Yellow *El Capitan* scheme; 1997	**159**	**225**

70′ Streamlined

5-Car Sets

		MSRP	Current
20-6500	Atlantic Coast Line 5-Car 70′ Aluminum Passenger Set Smooth-sided; Purple/Black; 1996	**399**	**600**
20-6501	Atlantic Coast Line 5-Car 70′ Aluminum Passenger Set Fluted ridges; Aluminum-plated; 1996	**399**	**425**

**Premier Line Amtrak 70′ Streamlined
5-Car Passenger Set: top to bottom**

20-6508 baggage 100
dome 9400
dome 9401
coach 4010
dome/observation "Silver View"
9300

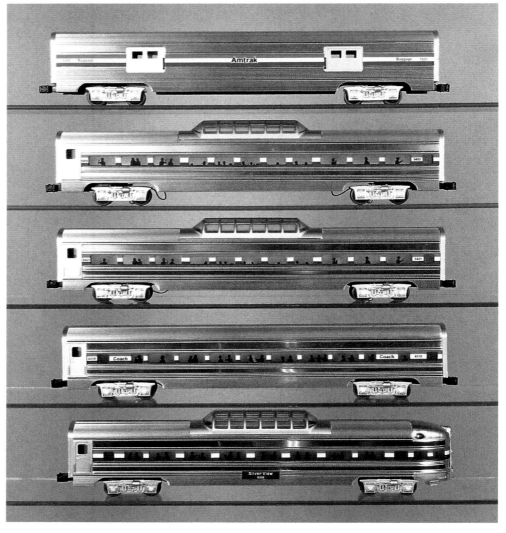

		MSRP	Current
20-6502	Chesapeake & Ohio 5-Car 70′ Aluminum Passenger Set; includes baggage car no. 314, coach 1611, coach 1632, and observation 2507 "Wolverine Club" Smooth-sided; Blue/Gray; 1996	399	430
20-6503	Southern 5-Car 70′ Aluminum Passenger Set Fluted ridges; Aluminum-plated; 1996	399	425
20-6504	New York Central 5-Car 70′ Aluminum Passenger Set Fluted ridges; Aluminum-plated; 1996	399	405
20-6505	Burlington 5-Car 70′ Aluminum Passenger Set Fluted ridges; Aluminum-plated; 1996	399	550
20-6506	Union Pacific 5-Car 70′ Aluminum Passenger Set Smooth-sided; Yellow/Gray; 1996	399	410

		MSRP	Current
20-6507	Pennsylvania RR 5-Car 70′ Aluminum Passenger Set Smooth-sided; Tuscan Red; 1997	399	405
20-6508	Amtrak 5-Car 70′ Aluminum Passenger Set; includes baggage car no. 100, dome 9400, dome 1632, coach 4010, and observation 9300 "Silver View" Fluted ridges; Silver; 1997	399	400
20-6509	New York Central 5-Car 70′ Aluminum Passenger Set Fluted ridges; Aluminum-plated; 1997	399	405
20-6510	Union Pacific 5-Car 70′ Aluminum Passenger Set Smooth-sided; Yellow; 1997	399	405
20-6511	Baltimore & Ohio 5-Car 70′ Aluminum Passenger Set Smooth-sided; Blue/Gray/Yellow *Cincinnatian* scheme; 1997	399	280

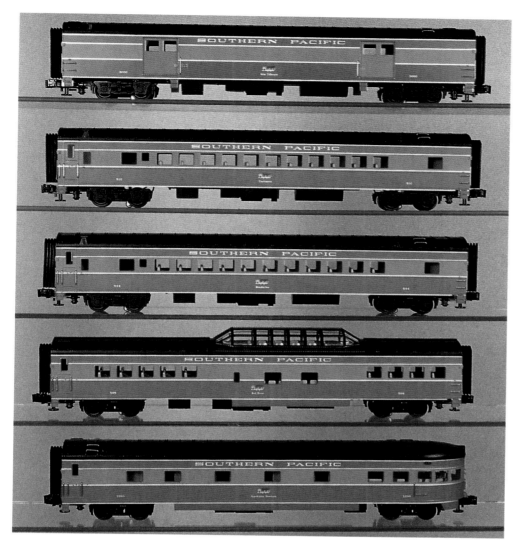

		MSRP	Current
20-6512	Rock Island 5-Car 70' ABS Passenger Set Fluted ridges; Red/Silver; 1997	**249**	**300**
20-6513	Baltimore & Ohio 5-Car 70' ABS Passenger Set Fluted ridges; Blue; 1997	**249**	**300**
20-6514	Norfolk & Western 5-Car 70' ABS Passenger Set Smooth-sided; Maroon; 1997	**249**	**300**
20-6515	Seaboard Coast Line 5-Car 70' ABS Passenger Set Fluted ridges; Brown; 1997	**249**	**300**
20-6516	New York Central 5-Car 70' ABS Passenger Set Smooth-sided; two-tone Gray; 1998	**250**	**240**
20-6517	Southern 5-Car 70' ABS Passenger Set Smooth-sided; Green/White; 1998	**250**	**250**

		MSRP	Current
20-6518	Alaska RR 5-Car 70' ABS Passenger Set Smooth-sided; Yellow/Blue; 1998	**250**	**250**
20-6523	Southern Pacific 5-Car 70' ABS Passenger Set; includes baggage car no. 3000 "Miln Gillespie," coach 510 "Tuolomne," coach 544 "Mendocino," dome 568 "Red River," and observation 1290 "Appekunny Mountain" Smooth-sided; Orange/Red/Black; 1998	**250**	**300**
20-6525	New Haven 70' ABS Passenger Coach Fluted ridges; Silver/Orange/Black; 1999	**55**	**CP**
20-6526	Nickel Plate 5-Car 70' ABS Passenger Set Fluted ridges; Blue/Gray; 1999	**250**	**CP**
20-6527	Lehigh Valley 5-Car 70' ABS Passenger Set Fluted ridges; Red/Black; 1999	**250**	**CP**

**Premier Line Amtrak 70′ Streamlined
2-Car Sleeper/Diner Set**
20-6608 "Pacific Forum" sleeper
diner 8555

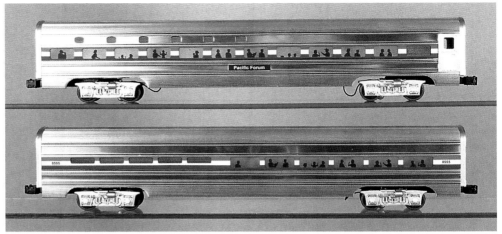

		MSRP	Current				MSRP	Current
20-6528	Missouri Pacific 5-Car 70′ ABS Passenger Set Fluted ridges; Silver/Red; 1999	250	CP		20-6604	New York Central 2-Car 70′ Aluminum Sleeper/Diner Set Fluted ridges; Aluminum-plated; 1996	199	195
20-6529	Southern Pacific 5-Car 70′ ABS Passenger Set Fluted ridges; Orange/Red; 1999	250	CP		20-6605	Burlington 2-Car 70′ Aluminum Sleeper/Diner Set Fluted ridges; Aluminum-plated; 1996	199	225
20-6530	Pennsylvania RR 5-Car 70′ ABS Passenger Set Fluted ridges; Silver/Tuscan Red; 1999	250	CP		20-6606	Union Pacific 2-Car 70′ Aluminum Sleeper/Diner Set Smooth-sided; Yellow/Gray; 1996	199	225
20-6535	Kansas City Southern 5-Car 70′ ABS Passenger Set Smooth-sided; Green/Silver; 1999	250	CP		20-6607	Pennsylvania RR 2-Car 70′ Aluminum Sleeper/Diner Set Smooth-sided; Tuscan Red; 1997	199	190
20-6534	Electro-Motive Division 5-Car 70′ ABS Passenger Set Smooth-sided; Lt. Blue/Silver; 1999	250	CP		20-6608	Amtrak 2-Car 70′ Aluminum Sleeper/Diner Set; includes sleeper car "Pacific Forum," and diner 8555 Fluted ridges; Silver; 1997	199	200
20-6533	Pere Marquette 5-Car 70′ ABS Passenger Set Smooth-sided; Blue/Silver; 1999	250	CP		20-6609	New York Central 2-Car 70′ Aluminum Sleeper/Diner Set Fluted ridges; Aluminum-plated; 1997	199	200
20-6536	Chicago & North Western 5-Car 70′ ABS Passenger Set Smooth-sided; Green; 1999	250	CP		20-6610	Union Pacific 2-Car 70′ Aluminum Sleeper/Diner Set Smooth-sided; Yellow; 1997	199	200
20-6538	Union Pacific 5-Car 70′ ABS Passenger Set Smooth-sided; Yellow; 1999	250	CP		20-6611	Baltimore & Ohio 2-Car 70′ Aluminum Sleeper/Diner Set Smooth-sided; Blue/Gray; 1997	199	225

2-Car Sets

		MSRP	Current				MSRP	Current
20-6600	Atlantic Coast Line 2-Car 70′ Aluminum Sleeper/Diner Set Smooth-sided; Purple/Black; 1996	199	250		20-6612	Rock Island 2-Car 70′ ABS Sleeper/Diner Passenger Set Fluted ridges; Red/Silver; 1998	100	125
20-6601	Atlantic Coast Line 2-Car 70′ Aluminum Sleeper/Diner Set Fluted ridges; Aluminum-plated; 1996	199	220		20-6613	Baltimore & Ohio 2-Car 70′ Aluminum Sleeper/Diner Set Fluted ridges; Blue/Gray/Yellow painted; 1998	100	125
20-6602	Chesapeake & Ohio 2-Car 70′ Aluminum Sleeper/Diner Set Smooth-sided; Blue/Gray; 1996	199	225		20-6614	Norfolk & Western 2-Car 70′ ABS Sleeper/Diner Passenger Set Fluted ridges; Maroon/Black/Gold; 1998	100	125
20-6603	Southern 2-Car 70′ Aluminum Sleeper/Diner Set Fluted ridges; Aluminum-plated; 1996	199	200					

20-6519 lounge cafe 33040
            coach 34104
            coach 34123
            coach 34138

		MSRP	Current
20-6615	Seaboard Coast Line 2-Car 70′ ABS Sleeper/Diner Passenger Set Fluted ridges; Brown; 1998	**100**	**125**
20-6616	New York Central 2-Car 70′ ABS Sleeper/Diner Passenger Set Smooth-sided; two-tone Gray; 1998	**100**	**110**
20-6617	Southern 2-Car 70′ ABS Sleeper/Diner Passenger Set Smooth-sided; Green/White; 1998	**100**	**110**
20-6618	Alaska RR 2-Car 70′ ABS Sleeper/Diner Passenger Set Smooth-sided; Blue/Yellow; 1998	**100**	**110**
20-6623	Southern Pacific 2-Car 70′ ABS Sleeper/Diner Passenger Set Smooth-sided; Orange/Red/Black; 1998	**100**	**110**
20-6625	New Haven 2-Car 70′ ABS Sleeper/Diner Passenger Set Fluted ridges; Silver/Orange/Black; 1999	**100**	**CP**

		MSRP	Current
20-6626	Nickel Plate 2-Car 70′ ABS Sleeper/Diner Passenger Set Fluted ridges; Blue/Gray; 1999	**100**	**CP**
20-6627	Lehigh Valley 2-Car 70′ ABS Sleeper/Diner Passenger Set Fluted ridges; Red/Black; 1999	**100**	**CP**
20-6628	Missouri Pacific 2-Car 70′ ABS Sleeper/Diner Passenger Set Fluted ridges; Red/Silver; 1999	**100**	**CP**
20-6629	Southern Pacific 2-Car 70′ ABS Sleeper/Diner Passenger Set Fluted ridges; Orange/Red/Black; 1999	**100**	**CP**
20-6630	Pennsylvania RR 2-Car 70′ ABS Sleeper/Diner Passenger Set Fluted ridges; Silver/Tuscan Red; 1999	**100**	**CP**
20-6633	Pere Marquette 2-Car 70′ ABS Sleeper/Diner Passenger Set Smooth-sided; Blue/Silver; 1999	**100**	**CP**
20-6634	Electro-Motive Division 2-Car 70' ABS Sleeper/Diner Passenger Set Smooth-sided; Lt. Blue/Silver; 1999	**100**	**CP**

Premier Line Amtrak Superliner 4-Car
Passenger Set: top to bottom
20-6524 cafe/dinette 43007
coach 44002
coach 44103
coach 44212

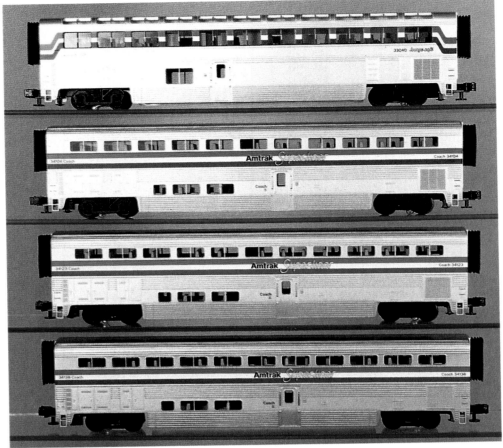

		MSRP	Current
20-6635	Kansas City Southern 2-Car 70′ ABS Sleeper/Diner Passenger Set Smooth-sided; Green/Silver; 1999	**100**	**CP**
20-6636	Chicago & North Western 2-Car 70′ ABS Sleeper/Diner Passenger Set Smooth-sided; Green; 1999	**100**	**CP**
20-6638	Union Pacific 2-Car 70′ ABS Sleeper/Diner Passenger Set Smooth-sided; Yellow; 1999	**100**	**CP**

Vista Domes

		MSRP	Current
20-6712	Rock Island 70′ ABS Full-Length Vista Dome Passenger Car Fluted ridges; Red/Silver; 1999	**60**	**CP**
20-6717	Southern Pacific 70′ ABS Full-Length Vista Dome Passenger Car Fluted ridges; Red/Orange; 1999	**60**	**CP**
20-6718	Alaska RR 70′ ABS Full-Length Vista Dome Passenger Car Smooth-sided; Blue/Yellow; 1999	**60**	**CP**

		MSRP	Current
20-6719	Southern Pacific 70′ ABS Full-Length Vista Dome Passenger Car Smooth-sided; Red/Orange/Black; 1999	**60**	**CP**
20-6729	Missouri-Kansas-Texas 70′ ABS Full-Length Vista Dome Passenger Car Fluted ridges; Silver/Red; 1999	**60**	**CP**

Amfleet

		MSRP	Current
20-6519	Amtrak 4-Car Amfleet Passenger Set; includes lounge cafe car no. 33040, coach 34104, coach 34123, and coach 34138 3 stripes; Silver/Red/Blue; 1998	**200**	**225**
20-6520	Metra 4-Car Amfleet Passenger Set Silver/Blue; 1998	**200**	**225**
20-6521	CalTran 4-Car Amfleet Passenger Set Silver/Teal; 1998	**200**	**225**
20-6522	Massachusetts Bay 4-Car Amfleet Passenger Set Silver/Purple; 1998	**200**	**225**

		MSRP	Current
20-6531	Amtrak 4-Car Amfleet Passenger Set 5 stripes; Silver/Red/Blue; 1999	**200**	**CP**
20-6532	SEPTA 4-Car Amfleet Passenger Set Silver/Blue/Red; 1999	**200**	**CP**

Superliner

4-Car Sets

		MSRP	Current
20-6524	Amtrak 4-Car Scale Superliner Set; includes cafe/dinette car no. 43007, coach 44002, coach 44103, and coach 44212 3 stripes; Silver; 1998	**250**	**275**
20-6537	Amtrak 4-Car Scale Superliner Set 5 stripes; Silver; 1999	**250**	**CP**

2-Car Sets

		MSRP	Current
20-6539	Amtrak 2-Car Superliner Sleeper/Diner Passenger Set 3 stripes; Silver; 1999	**126**	**CP**
20-6541	Amtrak 2-Car Superliner Sleeper/Diner Passenger Set 5 stripes; Silver; 1999	**126**	**CP**

Transitional Sleeper Cars

		MSRP	Current
20-6540	Amtrak Superliner Transitional Sleeper Passenger Car 3 stripes; Silver; 1999	**65**	**CP**
20-6542	Amtrak Superliner Transitional Sleeper Passenger Car 5 stripes; Silver; 1999	**65**	**CP**

RailKing Line
Steam Locomotives

RailKing steam engines have a lot of the appeal of their bigger brothers, but at about half the cost. Though not matching the Premier line in scale fidelity or level of detail, the heft of these smaller engines is still impressive, and the decoration is every bit as good as that of the "big boys." An impressive number of wheel configurations and chassis are available. Most RailKing steam engines are equipped with a die-cast chassis and tender, die-cast wheels, metal axles and gears, an electronic reversing unit, and a flywheel-equipped motor. Other features include operating headlight, operating coupler on the tender, smoke, and detailed cab interior. Proto-Sound is an available option.

Number 30-1139 Rail King Union Pacific 4-6-2 Forty-Niner Steam Locomotive 2906

30-1112 0-8-0 Four-Wheel Switcher Chicago & North Western 65

RailKing Line 0-8-0 Eight-Wheel Switchers: top to bottom
30-1111 0-8-0 Norfolk & Western Steam Switcher 244
30-1123 0-8-0 New York Central Steam Switcher 415
30-1124 0-8-0 Northern Pacific Steam Switcher 1189

		MSRP	Current
Four-Wheel Switcher (0-4-0)			
30–4026	Baltimore & Ohio 0-4-0 Steam Locomotive Ready-to-Run Train Set		
	Black; 1999		
	(–0) 3-Rail w/ Whistle	**150**	**CP**

		MSRP	Current
Eight-Wheel Switcher (0-8-0)			
30–1111	Norfolk & Western 0-8-0 Switcher Steam Locomotive numbered 244		
	Black; 1996		
	(–0) 3-Rail w/ Whistle	**299**	**300**
	(–1) 3-Rail w/ Proto-Sound	**379**	**400**
30–1112	Chicago & North Western 0-8-0 Switcher Steam Locomotive numbered 65		
	Black; 1996		
	(–0) 3-Rail w/ Whistle	**299**	**300**
	(–1) 3-Rail w/ Proto-Sound	**379**	**400**

30-Set 2-6-0 Mogul New York Central 2743
(from Sears Set)

30-1136 2-6-0 Mogul Santa Fe 605

		MSRP	Current
30–1123	New York Central 0-8-0 Switcher Steam Locomotive numbered 415 Black; 1997		
	(–0) 3-Rail w/ Whistle	299	300
	(–1) 3-Rail w/ Proto-Sound	399	385
30–1124	Northern Pacific 0-8-0 Switcher Steam Locomotive numbered 1189 Black; 1997		
	(–0) 3-Rail w/ Whistle	299	300
	(–1) 3-Rail w/ Proto-Sound	399	395
30–Set	Norfolk & Western 0-8-0 Steam Locomotive Ready-to-Run Coal Train Set Black; 1996		
	(–26) 3-Rail w/ Whistle	400	400
30–Set	Chicago & North Western 0-8-0 Steam Locomotive Ready-to-Run Freight Set Black; 1996		
	(–27) 3-Rail w/ Whistle	400	400

Mogul (2-6-0)

		MSRP	Current
30–Set	New York Central 2-6-0 Mogul Steam Locomotive (from Sears Set numbered 65808134022) numbered 2743; also includes 30-76120 MTH Construction Company flatcar, Timken Roller Bearing boxcar, and 30-7721 New York Central wood-sided caboose Black; 1998		
	(–0) 3-Rail w/ Whistle	N/A	N/A
	(–1) 3-Rail w/ Proto-Sound	N/A	N/A

		MSRP	Current
30–1136	Santa Fe 2-6-0 Mogul Steam Locomotive numbered 605 on Tender Black; 1999		
	(–0) 3-Rail w/ Whistle	130	CP
	(–1) 3-Rail w/ Proto-Sound	230	CP
30–1137	Baltimore & Ohio 2-6-0 Mogul Steam Locomotive Black; 1999		
	(–0) 3-Rail w/ Whistle	130	CP
	(–1) 3-Rail w/ Proto-Sound	230	CP
30–1148	Pennsylvania RR 2-6-0 Mogul Steam Locomotive Black; 1999		
	(–0) 3-Rail w/ Whistle	130	CP
	(–1) 3-Rail w/ Proto-Sound	230	CP
30–1150	Union Pacific 2-6-0 Mogul Steam Locomotive Black; 1999		
	(–0) 3-Rail w/ Whistle	130	CP
	(–1) 3-Rail w/ Proto-Sound	230	CP
30–4017	Santa Fe 2-6-0 Steam Locomotive Ready-to-Run Train Set Black; 1998		
	(–0) 3-Rail w/ Whistle	200	190
	(–1) 3-Rail w/ Proto-Sound	280	275
30–4020	Baltimore & Ohio 2-6-0 Steam Locomotive Ready-to-Run Train Set Black; 1998		
	(–0) 3-Rail w/ Whistle	200	200
	(–1) 3-Rail w/ Proto-Sound	280	275

30-1110 2-8-4 Berkshire Erie 3389

30-1128 2-8-4 Berkshire Chesapeake & Ohio 2744

RailKing Line Americans: top to bottom
30-1120-1 4-4-0 American Western & Atlantic "General" 3
30-1135-1 4-4-0 American Western & Atlantic "Texas" 49

	MSRP	Current
Consolidation (2-8-0)		
30–4023 Pennsylvania RR 2-8-0 Steam Locomotive Ready-to-Run Train Set Black; 1999 **(–0)** 3-Rail w/ Whistle	200	CP
30–4023 Pennsylvania RR 2-8-0 Steam Locomotive Ready-to-Run Train Set Black; 1999 **(–1)** 3-Rail w/ Proto-Sound	280	CP
Berkshire (2-8-4)		
30–Set Nickel Plate 2-8-4 Berkshire Steam Locomotive Ready-to-Run Train Set Black; 1996 **(–24)** 3-Rail w/ Whistle	400	400

	MSRP	Current
30–Set Erie 2-8-4 Berkshire Steam Locomotive Ready-to-Run Train Set Black; 1996 **(–25)** 3-Rail w/ Whistle	400	400
30–1109 Nickel Plate 2-8-4 Berkshire Steam Locomotive Black; 1996 **(–0)** 3-Rail w/ Whistle	300	350
30–1110 Erie 2-8-4 Berkshire Steam Locomotive numbered 3389 Black; 1996 **(–0)** 3-Rail w/ Whistle	300	350
30–1128 Chesapeake & Ohio 2-8-4 Berkshire Steam Locomotive Black; 1998 **(–0)** 3-Rail w/ Whistle **(–1)** 3-Rail w/ Proto-Sound	300 400	300 370

RailKing Line Pacifics: top to bottom
30-1118 4-6-2 Torpedo Pacific
Pennsylvania 3768
30-1125 4-6-2 PS-4 Pacific Southern
Crescent Limited 1396
30-1115 4-6-2 K-4s Pacific Pennsylvania
1361
30-1139 4-6-2 Forty-Niner Pacific Union
Pacific 2906

		MSRP	Current

American (4-4-0)

30–1120 Western & Atlantic 4-4-0 "General" American Steam Locomotive
Black/Red pilot, cab and drive wheels; 1997

	MSRP	Current
(–0) 3-Rail w/ Whistle	299	300
(–1) 3-Rail w/ Proto-Sound	399	399

30–1135 Western & Atlantic 4-4-0 "Texas" American Steam Locomotive
Black/Red pilot and drive wheels/Brown cab, trim, and Tender w/ Blue striping; 1998

	MSRP	Current
(–0) 3-Rail w/ Whistle	300	300
(–1) 3-Rail w/ Proto-Sound	400	400

30–1155 Wild Wild West 4-4-0 "Wanderer" American Steam Locomotive
Green/Black; 1999

	MSRP	Current
(–0) 3-Rail w/ Whistle	330	CP
(–1) 3-Rail w/ Proto-Sound	430	CP

Ten-Wheeler (4-6-0)

30–1141 Central RR of New Jersey 4-6-0 Camelback Steam Locomotive numbered 631
Black; 1999

	MSRP	Current
(–0) 3-Rail w/ Whistle	300	CP
(–1) 3-Rail w/ Proto-Sound	400	CP

30–1142 Reading 4-6-0 Camelback Steam Locomotive
Black; 1999

	MSRP	Current
(–0) 3-Rail w/ Whistle	300	CP
(–1) 3-Rail w/ Proto-Sound	400	CP

30–1153 Denver & Rio Grande 4-6-0 Ten-Wheeler Steam Locomotive
Black; 1999

	MSRP	Current
(–0) 3-Rail w/ Whistle	130	CP
(–1) 3-Rail w/ Proto-Sound	230	CP

30–1154 Chesapeake & Ohio 4-6-0 Ten-Wheeler Steam Locomotive
Black; 1999

	MSRP	Current
(–0) 3-Rail w/ Whistle	130	CP
(–1) 3-Rail w/ Proto-Sound	230	CP

Pacific (4-6-2)

30–1115* Pennsylvania RR 4-6-2 K-4s Pacific Steam Locomotive numbered 1361. *Reviewed in CTT December 1997*
Black; 1997

	MSRP	Current
(–0) 3-Rail w/ Whistle	300	325
(–1) 3-Rail w/ Proto-Sound	380	425

RailKing Line Hudsons: top to bottom

30-1103 4-6-4 Hudson New York Central 5405

30-1113 4-6-4 Dreyfuss Hudson New York Central 5445

30-1127 4-6-4 Hudson Milwaukee Road *Hiawatha* 100

30-1133 4-6-4 Hudson New York Central *Commodore Vanderbilt*

		MSRP	Current
30–1118*	Pennsylvania RR 4-6-2 Torpedo Pacific Steam Locomotive numbered 3768. *Reviewed in CTT December 1997* Black w/ Gold striping on Tender; 1997		
	(–0) 3-Rail w/ Whistle	299	325
	(–1) 3-Rail w/ Proto-Sound	399	399
30–1122	Denver & Rio Grande Western 4-6-2 Pacific Steam Locomotive Black; 1997		
	(–1) 3-Rail w/ Proto-Sound	399	375
30–1125	Southern 4-6-2 PS-4 Pacific Steam Locomotive Green/Silver smokebox and firebox; lettered "Crescent Limited" on Tender; 1997		
	(–0) 3-Rail w/ Whistle	299	325
	(–1) 3-Rail w/ Proto-Sound	399	425
30–1035	Denver & Rio Grande Western 4-6-2 Steam Locomotive Ready-to-Run Ski Train Set Black; 1997		
	(–) 3-Rail w/ Whistle	399	399
30–1138	Pennsylvania RR 4-6-2 K-4s Pacific Steam Locomotive numbered 1396 Black; 1998		
	(–0) 3-Rail w/ Whistle	300	300
	(–1) 3-Rail w/ Proto-Sound	400	400

		MSRP	Current
30–1139	Union Pacific 4-6-2 Forty-Niner Hudson Steam Locomotive numbered 2906 Brown/Yellow; 1998		
	(–0) 3-Rail w/ Whistle	330	350
	(–1) 3-Rail w/ Proto-Sound	430	450
30–1152	Reading 4-6-2 Crusader Hudson Steam Locomotive Silver/Blue; 1999		
	(–0) 3-Rail w/ Whistle	430	450
	(–1) 3-Rail w/ Proto-Sound	330	CP

Hudson (4-6-4)

		MSRP	Current
30–Set	New York Central 4-6-4 Hudson Steam Locomotive Ready-to-Run Train Set Black; 1996		
	(–17) 3-Rail w/ Whistle	400	400
30–Set	Union Pacific 4-6-4 Hudson Steam Locomotive Ready-to-Run Train Set Black; 1996		
	(–18) 3-Rail w/ Whistle	400	400
30–1025	New York Central 4-6-4 Hudson Steam Locomotive Ready-to-Run Train Set Black; 1997 or 1998		
	(–0) 3-Rail w/ Whistle	399	399

30-1101 4-8-2 Mohawk New York Central 3000

30-1114 4-8-2 Mohawk Texas & Pacific 907

		MSRP	Current
30–1103	New York Central 4-6-4 Hudson Steam Locomotive numbered 5405 Black; 1996		
	(–0) 3-Rail w/ Whistle	300	325
30–1104	Union Pacific 4-6-4 Hudson Steam Locomotive Black; 1996		
	(–0) 3-Rail w/ Whistle	300	300
30–1113	New York Central 4-6-4 Dreyfuss Hudson Steam Locomotive numbered 5445 Gray; 1996		
	(–0) 3-Rail w/ Whistle	330	375
	(–1) 3-Rail w/ Proto-Sound	399	475
30–1121	New York Central 4-6-4 Hudson Steam Locomotive numbered 5405 Black; 1999		
	(–0) 3-Rail w/ Whistle	299	300
	(–1) 3-Rail w/ Proto-Sound	399	399
30–1127*	Milwaukee Road *Hiawatha* 4-6-4 Hudson Steam Locomotive numbered 100. *Reviewed in CTT December 1998* Gray/Orange/Black; 1998		
	(–0) 3-Rail w/ Whistle	330	450
	(–1) 3-Rail w/ Proto-Sound	430	600
30–1133*	New York Central 4-6-4 *Commodore Vanderbilt* Hudson Steam Locomotive. *Reviewed in CTT July 1999* Dark Gray; 1998		
	(–0) 3-Rail w/ Whistle	330	330
	(–1) 3-Rail w/ Protosounds	430	390

		MSRP	Current
30–1143	New York Central 4-6-4 *Empire State Express* Hudson Steam Locomotive numbered 5426 Black/Gray; 1999		
	(–0) 3-Rail w/ Whistle	330	CP
	(–1) 3-Rail w/ Proto-Sound	430	CP
30–1146	New York Central 4-6-4 Hudson Steam Locomotive numbered 5412 Black; 1999		
	(–1) 3-Rail w/ Proto-Sound	400	CP
30–1147	Wabash 4-6-4 Streamlined Hudson Steam Locomotive Navy Blue; 1999		
	(–0) 3-Rail w/ Whistle	330	CP
	(–1) 3-Rail w/ Proto-Sound	430	CP

Mohawk (4-8-2)

		MSRP	Current
30–1101	New York Central 4-8-2 L-3 Mohawk Steam Locomotive numbered 3000 Black; 1995		
	(–) 3-Rail w/ Whistle	299	300
30–1102*	Santa Fe 4-8-2 L-3 Mohawk Steam Locomotive numbered 3700. *Reviewed in CTT February 1996* Black; 1995		
	(–) 3-Rail w/ Whistle	299	300
30–1114	Texas & Pacific 4-8-2 L-3 Mohawk Steam Locomotive numbered 907 Blue/Gray; 1997		
	(–0) 3-Rail w/ Whistle	300	325
	(–1) 3-Rail w/ Proto-Sound	379	470

Northern (4-8-4)

		MSRP	Current
30–1105	Norfolk & Western 4-8-4 J Northern Steam Locomotive numbered 611 Black; 1996		
	(–0) 3-Rail w/ Whistle	300	600

RailKing Line Northerns: top to bottom

30-1105 4-8-4 J Northern Norfolk & Western 611

30-1106 4-8-4 Northern Santa Fe "Blue Goose" 3760

30-1119 4-8-4 Northern Southern Pacific *Daylight* 4449

30-1140 4-8-4 Northern Santa Fe 2926

30-1131 4-8-4 GS-4 Northern National Biscuit Company 1898

		MSRP	Current
30–1106	Santa Fe 4-8-4 "Blue Goose" Northern Steam Locomotive numbered 3760 Two-tone Blue; 1996		
	(–0) 3-Rail w/ Whistle	300	700
30–1119	Southern Pacific 4-8-4 GS-4 Northern Steam Locomotive numbered 4449 Black/Orange; 1997		
	(–0) 3-Rail w/ Whistle	329	360
	(–1) 3-Rail w/ Proto-Sound	429	525

		MSRP	Current
30–1131	National Biscuit Company 4-8-4 Northern Steam Locomotive numbered 1898 on Tender Blue/Red; 1998		
	(–0) 3-Rail w/ Whistle	N/A	N/A
30–1140*	Santa Fe 4-8-4 Northern Steam Locomotive numbered 2926 on Tender and sandbox. *Reviewed in CTT October 1999* Black; 1998		
	(–0) 3-Rail w/ Whistle	330	350
	(–1) 3-Rail w/ Proto-Sound	430	450

30-1116 2-6-6-6 Allegheny Chesapeake & Ohio 1604

30-1129 4-8-8-4 Big Boy Union Pacific 4020

		MSRP	Current
30–1151	Union Pacific 4-8-4 FEF Northern Steam Locomotive Gray; 1999		
	(−0) 3-Rail w/ Whistle	330	CP
	(−1) 3-Rail w/ Proto-Sound	430	CP

Turbine (6-8-6)

		MSRP	Current
30–1149	Pennsylvania RR 6-8-6 S-2 Turbine Steam Locomotive Black; 1999		
	(−0) 3-Rail w/ Whistle	330	CP
	(−1) 3-Rail w/ Proto-Sound	430	CP

Allegheny (2-6-6-6)

		MSRP	Current
30–1116	Chesapeake & Ohio 2-6-6-6 Allegheny Steam Locomotive numbered 1604 Black; 1997		
	(−0) 3-Rail w/ Whistle	550	695
	(−1) 3-Rail w/ Proto-Sound	630	795

Challenger (4-6-6-4)

		MSRP	Current
30–1107	Union Pacific 4-6-6-4 Challenger Steam Locomotive Gray/Black; 1996		
	(−0) 3-Rail w/ Whistle	499	850
30–1108*	Union Pacific 4-6-6-4 Challenger Steam Locomotive numbered 3985. *Reviewed in CTT January 1997* Black; 1996		
	(−0) 3-Rail w/ Whistle	500	850

Cab-Forward (4-8-8-2)

		MSRP	Current
30–1144	Southern Pacific 4-8-8-2 Cab-Forward Steam Locomotive Black; 1999		
	(−0) 3-Rail w/ Whistle	600	CP
	(−1) 3-Rail w/ Proto-Sound	700	CP

Big Boy (4-8-8-4)

		MSRP	Current
30–1129	Union Pacific 4-8-8-4 Big Boy Steam Locomotive numbered 4020 Black; 1998		
	(−0) 3-Rail w/ Whistle	600	750
	(−1) 3-Rail w/ Proto-Sound	700	900

Auxiliary Water Tenders

		MSRP	Current
30–1117	N&W Auxiliary Fuel Tender Black w/ Maroon striping; 1997	129	150
30–1126	SP Auxiliary Fuel Tender Orange; 1997	129	125
30–1130	UP Auxiliary Water Tender Yellow; 1998	130	130

RailKing Line
Diesels, Electric Locomotives, & Motorized Units

RailKing diesels (including electrics) are available in an impressive variety of models and roadnames. While not exact ¼″ scale, they are aesthetically appropriate in their major proportions, making them suitable for service with smaller freight cars and passenger cars from MTH or other manufacturers. The ABS bodies are rugged, and the locomotives ride on die-cast trucks, carry die-cast operating couplers, have operating headlights, an electronic reverse unit, handsome decoration, and an impressive level of detail. Proto-Sound versions are available as indicated in the listings that follow.

Number 30-2121 RailKing Santa Fe SD90MAC Diesel Locomotive 8300

30-2004 Dash 8-40B Santa Fe 560

30-2114 Dash 8-40C Norfolk Southern 8763

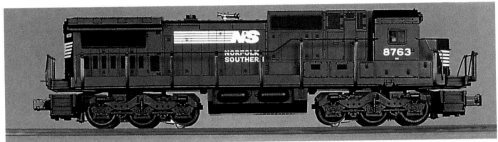

		MSRP	Current

Dash 8-40

		MSRP	Current
30–1015	Norfolk Southern Dash 8-40C Diesel Locomotive Ready-to-Run Unit Train Set Black; 1997		
	(–) 3-Rail w/ Horn	299	285
30–2003*	Amtrak Dash 8-40B Diesel Locomotive numbered 500. *Reviewed in CTT February 1997* Silver/Red/Blue; 1996		
	(–) 3-Rail w/ Horn	179	225
30–2004	Santa Fe Dash 8-40B Diesel Locomotive numbered 560 Silver/Red; 1996		
	(–) 3-Rail w/ Horn	179	225
30–2114	Norfolk Southern Dash 8-40C Diesel Locomotive numbered 8763 Black; 1997		
	(–0) 3-Rail w/ Horn	179	140
	(–1) 3-Rail w/ Proto-Sound	279	255
30–2115	Santa Fe Dash 8-40B Diesel Locomotive Blue/Yellow; 1997		
	(–0) 3-Rail w/ Horn	179	170
	(–1) 3-Rail w/ Proto-Sound	279	260
30–2129	Burlington Northern Santa Fe Dash 8-40B Diesel Locomotive Green/Orange; 1998		
	(–0) 3-Rail w/ Horn	130	150
	(–1) 3-Rail w/ Proto-Sound	230	230

		MSRP	Current
30–2136	Conrail Dash 8-40B Diesel Locomotive Blue/White; 1998		
	(–0) 3-Rail w/ Horn	130	150
	(–1) 3-Rail w/ Proto-Sound	230	200
30–2155	Chicago & North Western Dash 8-40C Diesel Locomotive Green/Yellow; 1999		
	(–0) 3-Rail w/ Horn	130	CP
	(–1) 3-Rail w/ Proto-Sound	230	CP
30–2164	Amtrak Dash 8 Diesel Locomotive Ready-to-Run Passenger Train Set Silver/Red/Blue; 1999		
	(–1) 3-Rail w/ Proto-Sound	350	CP
30–4019	Conrail Dash 8-40B Diesel Locomotive Ready-to-Run Work Train Set Blue; 1998		
	(–0) 3-Rail w/ Horn	250	240
	(–1) 3-Rail w/ Proto-Sound	321	300
30–4024	Amtrak Dash 8 Diesel Locomotive Ready-to-Run Work Train Set Silver/Red/Blue; 1999		
	(–0) 3-Rail w/ Horn	250	CP
	(–1) 3-Rail w/ Proto-Sound	330	CP

E8 AA

		MSRP	Current
30–2140*	New York Central E8 AA Diesel Locomotive Set numbered 4084 and 4045. *Reviewed in CTT October 1999* Two-tone Gray 1999		
	(–0) 3-Rail w/ Horn	180	CP
	(–1) 3-Rail w/ Proto-Sound	280	CP

30-2001 F3AA New York Central 1607,1606

		MSRP	Current
30–2141	Southern Pacific E8 AA Diesel Locomotive Set numbered 6046 and 6018 Red/Orange; 1999		
	(**–0**) 3-Rail w/ Horn	**180**	**CP**
	(**–1**) 3-Rail w/ Proto-Sound	**280**	**CP**

E8 B

		MSRP	Current
30–2140	New York Central E8 B-Unit Diesel Locomotive numbered 4109 Two-tone Gray; 1999		
	(**–3**) 3-Rail non-powered	**60**	**CP**
30–2141	Southern Pacific E8 B-Unit Diesel Locomotive numbered 6002B Red/Orange; 1999		
	(**–3**) 3-Rail non-powered	**60**	**CP**

F3 AA

		MSRP	Current
30–2001	New York Central F3 AA Diesel Locomotive Set numbered 1606 and 1607 Two-tone Gray; 1998		
	(**–0**) 3-Rail w/ Horn	**200**	**250**
30–2002	Union Pacific F3 AA Diesel Locomotive Set Yellow/Gray; 1996		
	(**–0**) 3-Rail w/ Horn	**200**	**250**
30–2007*	Florida East Coast F3 AA Diesel Locomotive Set numbered 503 and 504. *Reviewed in CTT September 1997* Yellow/Red; 1998		
	(**–0**) 3-Rail w/ Horn	**199**	**180**
	(**–1**) 3-Rail w/ Horn	**279**	**280**

RailKing Line F3s A's and B: left to right, top to bottom
30-2130 F3 AA Pennsylvania 9505, 9507
30-2132 F3 B Unit Pennsylvania

RailKing Line F3s A and B: top to bottom
30-2137 F3 A Santa Fe 17
30-2133 F3 B Unit Santa Fe

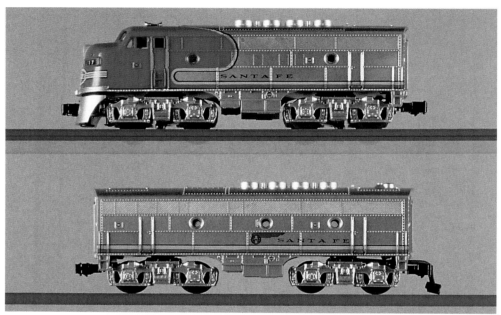

		MSRP	Current			MSRP	Current
30–2008	Western Pacific F3 AA Diesel Locomotive Set numbered 301 and 302 Silver/Orange; 1997			30–2131	Santa Fe F3 AA Diesel Locomotive Set numbered 16 and 17 Silver/Red; 1998		
	(−0) 3-Rail w/ Horn	199	200		(−0) 3-Rail w/ Horn	180	180
	(−1) 3-Rail w/ Proto-Sound	279	280		(−1) 3-Rail w/ Proto-Sound	280	300
30–2118	Chessie F3 A Diesel Locomotive numbered 4321 Yellow/Blue; 1997			30–2137	Santa Fe F3 A Unit numbered 17 Silver/Red; 1998		
	(−) 3-Rail non-powered	60	60		(−) 3-Rail non-powered	60	60
30–2130	Pennsylvania RR F3 AA Diesel Locomotive Set numbered 9505 and 9507 Tuscan Red w/ 5 Gold stripes; 1998			30–2142	Electro-Motive Division F3 AA Diesel Locomotive Set Blue/Silver; 1999		
	(−0) 3-Rail w/ Horn	180	180		(−0) 3-Rail w/ Horn	160	CP
	(−1) 3-Rail w/ Proto-Sound	280	300		(−1) 3-Rail w/ Proto-Sound	260	CP
				30–2143	Baltimore & Ohio F3 AA Diesel Locomotive Set Blue/Gray; 1999		
					(−0) 3-Rail w/ Horn	160	CP
					(−1) 3-Rail w/ Proto-Sound	260	CP

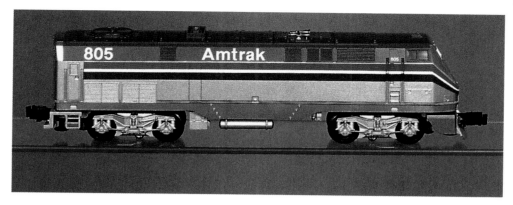

		MSRP	Current
30–Set	New York Central F3 A Diesel Locomotive Freight Set Two-tone Gray; 1996		
	(−19)	300	300
30–Set	Union Pacific F3 A Diesel Locomotive Freight Set Yellow/Gray; 1996		
	(−20)	300	300
30–4016*	Chessie F3 A Diesel Locomotive Ready-to-Run Construction Set numbered 4320. *Reviewed in CTT January 1998* Yellow/Blue; 1997		
	(−0) 3-Rail w/ Horn	200	200
	(−1) 3-Rail w/ Proto-Sound	280	280
30–4021	Santa Fe F3 A Diesel Locomotive Ready-to-Run Passenger Train Set Silver/Red; 1998		
	(−0) 3-Rail w/ Horn	230	300
	(−1) 3-Rail w/ Proto-Sound	310	325

F3 B

		MSRP	Current
30–2010	New York Central F3 B Unit Two-tone Gray; 1997		
	(−3) 3-Rail non-powered	80	80
30–2011	Union Pacific F3 B Unit Yellow/Gray; 1997		
	(−3) 3-Rail non-powered	80	80
30–2012*	Florida East Coast F3 B Unit numbered 552. *Reviewed in CTT September 1997* Yellow/Red; 1997		
	(−3) 3-Rail non-powered	80	80
30–2013	Western Pacific F3 B Unit Silver/Orange; 1997		
	(−3) 3-Rail non-powered	80	60

		MSRP	Current
30–2119	Chessie F3 B Unit Blue/Gray; 1997		
	(−) 3-Rail non-powered	50	60
30–2132	Pennsylvania RR F3 B Unit Tuscan Red w/ 5 Gold stripes; 1998		
	(−) 3-Rail non-powered	60	60
30–2133	Santa Fe F3 B Unit Silver/Red; 1998		
	(−) 3-Rail non-powered	60	60
30–2142	Electro-Motive Division F3 B Unit Blue/Silver; 1999		
	(−3) 3-Rail non-powered	50	CP
30–2143	Baltimore & Ohio F3 B Unit Blue/Gray; 1999		
	(−3) 3-Rail non-powered	50	CP

F40PH

		MSRP	Current
30–4025	Amtrak F40PH Diesel Locomotive Ready-to-Run Passenger Train Set Silver/Red/Blue; 1999		
	(−0) 3-Rail w/ Horn	250	CP
	(−1) 3-Rail w/ Proto-Sound	330	CP

Genesis

		MSRP	Current
30–2160	Amtrak Genesis Diesel Locomotive numbered 805 Silver/Red/Blue; 1999		
	(−0) 3-Rail w/ Horn	130	CP
	(−1) 3-Rail w/ Proto-Sound	230	CP
30–4018*	Amtrak Genesis Diesel Locomotive Ready-to-Run Train Set. *Reviewed in CTT February 1999* Silver/Red/Blue; 1998		
	(−0) 3-Rail w/ Horn	300	300
	(−1) 3-Rail w/ Proto-Sound	380	400

30-2138 NW2 Switcher Union Pacific
D.S.1050

		MSRP	Current
H-24-66 Train Master			
30–Set	Santa Fe Train Master Freight Set Silver/Red; 1996		
	(–21)	380	380
NW2			
30–2138	Union Pacific NW2 Diesel Locomotive Switcher numbered D.S.1050 Yellow/Gray lettered "Road of the Streamliners"; 1998		
	(–0) 3-Rail w/ Horn	130	130
	(–1) 3-Rail w/ Proto-Sound	230	230
	(–3) 3-Rail non-powered Calf numbered D.S.1050B	50	50
30–2139	Chicago & North Western NW2 Diesel Locomotive Switcher numbered 1017 Yellow/Green; 1998		
	(–0) 3-Rail w/ Horn	130	130
	(–1) 3-Rail w/ Proto-Sound	230	230
	(–3) 3-Rail non-powered Calf	50	50
30–2156	Santa Fe NW2 Diesel Locomotive Switcher numbered 1105 Black/White; 1999		
	(–0) 3-Rail w/ Horn	130	CP
	(–1) 3-Rail w/ Proto-Sound	230	CP
	(–3) 3-Rail non-powered Calf	50	CP
30–2157	Southern NW2 Diesel Locomotive Switcher Green/White; 1999		
	(–0) 3-Rail w/ Horn	130	CP
	(–1) 3-Rail w/ Proto-Sound	230	CP
	(–3) 3-Rail non-powered	50	CP
PA-1			
30–2125	Delaware & Hudson Alco PA AA Diesel Locomotive Set Blue/Silver; 1998		
	(–0) 3-Rail w/ Horn	180	200
	(–1) 3-Rail w/ Proto-Sound	280	300

		MSRP	Current
30–2126	Denver & Rio Grande Western Alco PA AA Diesel Locomotive Set numbered 6011 and 6003 Yellow/Silver; 1998		
	(–0) 3-Rail w/ Horn	180	200
	(–1) 3-Rail w/ Proto-Sound	280	285
30–2150	Santa Fe Alco PA AA Diesel Locomotive Set Silver/Red; 1999		
	(–0) 3-Rail w/ Horn	180	CP
	(–1) 3-Rail w/ Proto-Sound	280	CP
30–2151	Southern Alco PA AA Diesel Locomotive Set Green/White; 1999		
	(–0) 3-Rail w/ Horn	180	CP
	(–1) 3-Rail w/ Proto-Sound	280	CP
PB-1			
30–2127	Delaware & Hudson Alco PA B Unit Blue/Silver; 1998		
	(–) 3-Rail non-powered	60	60
30–2128	Denver & Rio Grande Western Alco PA B Unit Yellow/Silver; 1998		
	(–) 3-Rail non-powered	60	60
30–2150	Santa Fe Alco PA B Unit Silver/Red; 1999		
	(–3) 3-Rail non-powered	60	CP
30–2151	Southern Alco PA B Unit Green; 1999		
	(–3) 3-Rail non-powered	60	CP
SD45			
30–2152	Union Pacific SD45 Diesel Locomotive Yellow/Gray; 1999		
	(–0) 3-Rail w/ Horn	130	CP
	(–1) 3-Rail w/ Proto-Sound	230	CP
30–2153	Pennsylvania RR SD45 Diesel Locomotive Tuscan Red; 1999		
	(–0) 3-Rail w/ Horn	130	CP
	(–1) 3-Rail w/ Proto-Sound	230	CP

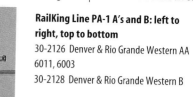
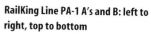

RailKing Line PA-1 A's and B: left to right, top to bottom
30-2126 Denver & Rio Grande Western AA 6011, 6003
30-2128 Denver & Rio Grande Western B

30-2006 SD60 Chicago & North Western 8029

SD60

		MSRP	Current
30–Set	Conrail SD60 Freight Set Blue/White; 1996 (–28)	270	270
30–Set	Chicago & North Western SD60 Diesel Locomotive Freight Set Yellow/Green; 1996 (–29)	270	270
30–2005	Conrail SD60 Diesel Locomotive Blue/White; 1996 (–0) 3-Rail w/ Horn (–1) 3-Rail w/ Proto-Sound	180 260	180 260
30–2006	Chicago & North Western SD60 Diesel Locomotive numbered 8029 Yellow/Green lettered "Operation Lifesaver" on hood and "Look, Listen…and Live" on cab; 1996 (–0) 3-Rail w/ Horn (–1) 3-Rail w/ Proto-Sound	180 260	180 260
30–2116	CSX SD60M Diesel Locomotive Blue/Gray; 1997 (–0) 3-Rail w/ Horn (–1) 3-Rail w/ Proto-Sound	179 279	200 265
30–2117	Union Pacific SD60M Diesel Locomotive numbered 6365 Yellow/Gray; 1997 (–0) 3-Rail w/ Horn (–1) 3-Rail w/ Proto-Sound	179 279	210 265

SD90

		MSRP	Current
30–2120	Conrail SD90MAC Diesel Blue/White; 1998 (–0) 3-Rail w/ Horn (–1) 3-Rail w/ Proto-Sound	130 230	130 225
30–2121	Santa Fe SD90MAC Diesel Locomotive numbered 8300 Silver/Red Warbonnet scheme; 1998 (–0) 3-Rail w/ Horn (–1) 3-Rail w/ Proto-Sound	130 230	130 225

SW8

		MSRP	Current
30–2146	Atlantic Coast Line SW8 Diesel Locomotive Switcher Purple/Silver; 1999 (–0) 3-Rail w/ Horn (–1) 3-Rail w/ Proto-Sound	130 230	CP CP
30–2147	Erie-Lackawanna SW8 Diesel Locomotive Switcher Maroon/Gray; 1999 (–0) 3-Rail w/ Horn (–1) 3-Rail w/ Proto-Sound	130 230	CP CP
30–2165	Chicago & North Western SW8 Switcher Diesel Locomotive Yellow/Green; 1999 (–0) 3-Rail w/ Horn (–1) 3-Rail w/ Proto-Sound	130 230	CP CP
30–2166	CP Rail SW8 Switcher Diesel Locomotive Red; 1999 (–0) 3-Rail w/ Horn (–1) 3-Rail w/ Proto-Sound	130 230	CP CP

30-2009 Gas-Turbine Union Pacific 10, 10B
Tender Union Pacific 10

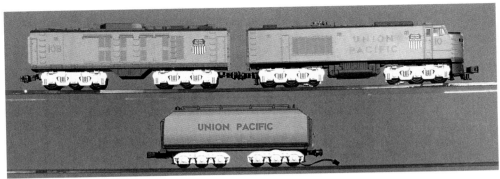

		MSRP	Current
SW9			
30–2148	Western Pacific SW9 Diesel Locomotive Switcher Silver/Orange; 1999		
	(–0) 3-Rail w/ Horn	130	CP
	(–1) 3-Rail w/ Proto-Sound	230	CP
30–2149	Pennsylvania RR SW9 Diesel Locomotive Switcher Black; 1999		
	(–0) 3-Rail w/ Horn	130	CP
	(–1) 3-Rail w/ Proto-Sound	230	CP
30–2167	Union Pacific SW9 Switcher Diesel Locomotive Yellow/Gray; 1999		
	(–0) 3-Rail w/ Horn	130	CP
	(–1) 3-Rail w/ Proto-Sound	230	CP
30–2168	Chesapeake & Ohio SW9 Switcher Diesel Locomotive Blue/Yellow; 1999		
	(–0) 3-Rail w/ Horn	130	CP
	(–1) 3-Rail w/ Proto-Sound	230	CP
30–2169	Burlington Northern Santa Fe SW9 Switcher Diesel Locomotive Green/Orange; 1999		
	(–0) 3-Rail w/ Horn	130	CP
	(–1) 3-Rail w/ Proto-Sound	230	CP
Gas-Turbine			
30–2009	Union Pacific Gas-Turbine Diesel Locomotive and Auxiliary Water Tender numbered 10 and 10B; Tender numbered 10 also Yellow/Gray; 1997		
	(–0) 3-Rail w/ Horn	399	300
	(–1) 3-Rail w/ Proto-Sound	479	399
EP-5			
30–2170	New Haven EP-5 Electric Locomotive Red/White/Black; 1999		
	(–0) 3-Rail w/ Horn	150	CP
	(–1) 3-Rail w/ Proto-Sound	250	CP

		MSRP	Current
30–2171	Great Northern EP-5 Electric Locomotive Green/Orange; 1999		
	(–0) 3-Rail w/ Horn	150	CP
	(–1) 3-Rail w/ Proto-Sound	250	CP
GG-1			
30–Set	Pennsylvania RR GG-1 Freight Set Tuscan Red; 1996		
	(–22)	400	400
30–Set	Pennsylvania RR GG-1 Freight Set Brunswick Green; 1996		
	(–23)	400	400
30–2500	Pennsylvania RR GG-1 Electric Locomotive Brunswick Green; 1996		
	(–) 3-Rail	299	325
30–2501	Pennsylvania RR GG-1 Electric Locomotive numbered 4913 Tuscan Red w/ 5 Gold stripes; 1996		
	(–) 3-Rail	299	325
30–2502	Amtrak GG-1 Electric Locomotive numbered 926 Silver/Red/Blue; 1996		
	(–) 3-Rail	299	270
30–2506	Pennsylvania RR GG-1 Electric Locomotive Brunswick Green; 1998		
	(–) 3-Rail	300	300
30–2507	Pennsylvania RR GG-1 Electric Locomotive Tuscan Red; 1998		
	(–) 3-Rail	300	300
30–5100	Pennsylvania RR GG-1 Electric Locomotive Brunswick Green; 1995		
	(–0) 3-Rail	299	425
30–5101	Pennsylvania RR GG-1 Electric Locomotive Tuscan Red; 1995		
	(–) 3-Rail	299	340

RailKing Line GG1s: top to bottom
30-5105 GG1 Pennsylvania Brunswick Green w/ 5 Gold stripes 4935
30-5104 GG1 Pennsylvania Silver w/ solid Tuscan stripe 4872
30-2502 GG1 Amtrak Silver/Red/Blue 926

		MSRP	Current
30–5102	Pennsylvania RR GG-1 Electric Locomotive Brunswick Green; 1995 (–) 3-Rail	299	400
30–5103	Pennsylvania RR GG-1 Electric Locomotive Brunswick Green; 1995 (–) 3-Rail	299	425
30–5104	Pennsylvania RR GG-1 Electric Locomotive numbered 4872 Silver w/ single Tuscan Red stripe; 1995 (–) 3-Rail	299	315
30–5105	Pennsylvania RR GG-1 Electric Locomotive numbered 4935 Brunswick Green w/ 5 Gold stripes; 1995 (–) 3-Rail	299	360

Hand Cars

		MSRP	Current
30–2508	Operating Hand Car Black; 1999 (–) 3-Rail	60	65

		MSRP	Current
30–2511	Operating Santa Claus Hand Car N/A; 1999 (–) 3-Rail	60	CP

Rotary Snow Plow

		MSRP	Current
30–2123	Denver & Rio Grande Western Rotary Snow Plow Silver; 1998 (–) 3-Rail	60	60
30–2124	Pennsylvania RR Rotary Snow Plow Yellow/Silver; 1998 (–) 3-Rail	60	60
30–7921	Chicago & North Western Rotary Snow Plow Yellow; 1999 (–) 3-Rail	60	CP
30–7922	Canadian National Rotary Snow Plow Orange; 1999 (–) 3-Rail	60	CP

Trolley Cars

		MSRP	Current
30–4027	Baltimore & Ohio Trolley Ready-to-Run Train Set Red/White; 1999 (–0) 3-Rail	100	CP

30-2134 Doodlebug Baltimore & Ohio 6005

30-2135 Doodlebug Santa Fe M.131

		MSRP	Current
30–4028	Holiday Special Trolley Ready-to-Run Train Set Green/Red lettered "Merry Christmas"; 1999		
	(–0) 3-Rail	100	CP

Galloping Goose
		MSRP	Current
30–2154	Denver & Rio Grande Western Galloping Goose Silver; 1999		
	(–0) 3-Rail w/ Horn	150	CP
	(–1) 3-Rail w/ Proto-Sound	250	CP

Doodlebug
		MSRP	Current
30–2134	Baltimore & Ohio Doodlebug numbered 6005 Blue/Gray; 1998		
	(–0) 3-Rail w/ Horn	120	120
	(–1) 3-Rail w/ Proto-Sound	220	220
30–2135*	Santa Fe Doodlebug numbered M.131. *Reviewed in CTT July 1999* Green/Red; 1998		
	(–0) 3-Rail w/ Horn	120	120
	(–1) 3-Rail w/ Proto-Sound	220	220
30–2158	Pennsylvania RR Doodlebug Tuscan Red; 1999		
	(–0) 3-Rail w/ Horn	120	CP
	(–1) 3-Rail w/ Proto-Sound	220	CP
30–2159	Chicago & North Western Doodlebug Green/Yellow; 1999		
	(–0) 3-Rail w/ Horn	120	CP
	(–1) 3-Rail w/ Proto-Sound	220	CP

PCC Electric Street Car
		MSRP	Current
30–2503	SEPTA PCC Electric Street Car numbered 2165 Gold/White; 1996		
	(–) 3-Rail	100	129

		MSRP	Current
30–2504*	San Francisco PCC Electric Street Car numbered 1050. *Reviewed in CTT July 1998* Green/White; 1997		
	(–0) 3-Rail	99	105
	(–1) 3-Rail w/ Proto-Sound	199	180
30–2505	Pittsburgh PCC Electric Street Car numbered 1713 Red/Cream; 1998		
	(–0) 3-Rail	100	110
	(–1) 3-Rail w/ Proto-Sound	200	175
30–2510	Washington PCC Electric Street Car White/Teal lettered "Silver Sightseer"; 1999		
	(–0) 3-Rail w/ Horn	100	CP
	(–1) 3-Rail w/ Proto-Sound	230	CP

Subway Cars
		MSRP	Current
30–2122	New York Transit 4-Car Subway Set numbered 4698, 4699, 4714, and 4715 Silver/Blue lettered "D" "205 Street Bronx Coney Island Brooklyn" with New York City "M" Transit logo; 1998		
	(–0) 3-Rail w/ Horn	200	315
	(–1) 3-Rail w/ Proto-Sound	300	315
30–2162	New York Transit 4-Car Subway Set Silver; 1999		
	(–0) 3-Rail w/ Horn	200	CP
	(–1) 3-Rail w/ Proto-Sound	300	CP
30–2161	New York Transit 2-Car Subway Add-On Silver/Blue; 1999		
	(–) 3-Rail non-powered	80	CP
30–2163	New York Transit 2-Car Subway Add-On Silver; 1999		
	(–) 3-Rail non-powered	80	CP

30-2503 PCC Electric SEPTA 2165

30-2122 Subway Cars NY Transit 4-Car Set
4698, 4699, 4714, 4715

	MSRP	Current
Rail Diesel Cars		
30–2144 Baltimore & Ohio Budd RDC Set		
Silver; 1999		
(–0) 3-Rail w/ Horn	**180**	**CP**
(–1) 3-Rail w/ Proto-Sound	**280**	**CP**

	MSRP	Current
30–2145 Santa Fe Budd Budd RDC Set		
Silver/Red; 1999		
(–0) 3-Rail w/ Horn	**180**	**CP**
(–1) 3-Rail w/ Proto-Sound	**280**	**CP**

W. 10-5   I. U. 7-5   E. W. 9-11   H. 12-11

40-6   I. W. 9-2   I. H. 10-0   CU.FT. 3703

8-35   X31A   P. R. R.

RailKing Line
Rolling Stock

RailKing freight cars, though categorized as "semi-scale," are beautiful pieces of craftsmanship that, like the locomotives, look great even though they are undersized. These railroad workhorses feature precisely molded cast-metal bodies that ride on die-cast sprung trucks and have die-cast operating couplers. The trucks feature needle-point axles and fast-angle metal wheels. Paint schemes are crisp and decoration accurately represents the railroads featured. Cars range from flatcars with loads; through flatcars, hoppers, and gondolas (with loads); to tank cars, boxcars, and cabooses. The variety of choices—and eras (from early steam to modern)—is impressive.

Number 30-7418 Pennsylvania RR Rounded-Roof Boxcar, 30-7620 Flatcar with Road Grader Load

RailKing Line Boxcars: left to right, top to bottom

30-7401 New York Central Boxcar 180190,
30-7407 New York Central "Pacemaker"
Boxcar 174020
30-7414 New York Central Peoria & Eastern
Boxcar 4503, 30-7423 MTH Railroader's
Club Boxcar
N/A Timken Roller Bearing Boxcar 60368
TRB (from Sears Set)

RailKing Line Christmas Cars: left to right, top to bottom

30-7805 Christmas 1995 Reefer, 30-7410
Christmas 1996 Boxcar
30-7416 Christmas 1997 Boxcar, 30-7426
Christmas 1998 Boxcar

Boxcars, Refrigerator Cars, and Stock Cars

Boxcars

		MSRP	Current
30-N/A	Timken Roller Bearing Boxcar numbered 60368 TRB (exclusive to Sears Set) Mustard/White; 1998	**N/A**	**N/A**
30-7400	Pennsylvania RR Boxcar numbered 47011 Tuscan Red; 1995	**28**	**20**
30-7401	New York Central Boxcar (also see 30-7415 below) numbered 180190 Tuscan Red; 1995	**28**	**35**
30-7402	Union Pacific Boxcar numbered 150231 Tuscan Red; 1995	**28**	**23**
30-7403	Santa Fe Boxcar numbered 20860 Tuscan Red; 1995	**28**	**28**
30-7404	Illinois Central Boxcar numbered 22094 Tuscan Red; 1995	**28**	**21**

		MSRP	Current
30-7405	Union Pacific Boxcar Yellow lettered "Automated Railway"; 1996	**28**	**28**
30-7406	Santa Fe Boxcar numbered 37625 Red/Black lettered "Shock Control"; 1996	**28**	**28**
30-7407	New York Central Boxcar numbered 174020 Red/Gray lettered "Pacemaker"; 1996	**28**	**25**
30-7408	Pennsylvania RR Boxcar numbered 28051 Tuscan Red/Silver lettered "Merchandise Service"; 1996	**28**	**26**
30-7409	RailBox Boxcar Yellow; 1996	**28**	**28**
30-7410	1996 Christmas Boxcar White/Gold with Christmas tree graphics lettered "MTH 1996" on door tackboard; 1996	**30**	**37**

30-7415 Oreo Cookie Boxcar (30-7401 on the box)

		MSRP	Current
30-7411	Chesapeake & Ohio Boxcar Blue lettered "C and O for Progress"; 1997	30	25
30-7412	Union Pacific Boxcar Brown lettered "Be Specific—ship UNION PACIFIC"; 1997	30	25
30-7413	Texas & Pacific Boxcar numbered 41200 Brown; 1997	33	29
30-7414	New York Central Boxcar numbered 4503 Jade Green lettered "Peoria & Eastern 'Quicker to Peoria'"; 1997	33	26
30-7415	Oreo Cookie Boxcar numbered NAB 031797 (30-7401 on box) Blue lettered "Oreo/America's Favorite Cookie/Celebrating 85 Years!"; 1998	33	N/A
30-7416	1997 Christmas Boxcar Dark Blue/White with Wise Men and angel graphics lettered "Peace on Earth" and "MTH 1997" on door tackboard;1997	33	33
30-7417	Chessie System Boxcar numbered 26621 Blue /Silver lettered "Chessie System"; 1997	33	33
30-7420	Union Pacific Boxcar numbered 4031 Yellow lettered "Road of the 'Big Boys'"; 1998	33	36
30-7421	Amtrak Boxcar numbered 1670 Silver; 1998	33	28
30-7422	Arrow Stapler Boxcar numbered 12509 Tuscan Red lettered "Genuine Arrow Staples"; 1998	33	33

		MSRP	Current
30-7423	MTH Railroader's Club Boxcar Purple/Silver with RailKing logo; 1998	N/A	N/A
30-7425	Big MO Boxcar Orange; 1998	N/A	CP
30-7426	1998 Christmas Boxcar Blue/White with Wise Men and Bethlehem graphics lettered "Joy to the World" and "MTH 1998" on door tackboard; 1998	33	28
30-7427	Atlantic Coast Line Boxcar Silver/Purple; 1999	33	CP
30-7428	Erie-Lackawanna Boxcar Brown; 1999	33	CP
30-7431	Santa Fe Boxcar Brown; 1999	33	CP
30-7434	1999 Holiday Boxcar Blue; 1999	33	CP
30-7437	Pennsylvania RR Boxcar Brown; 1999	33	CP
30-7438	Reading Boxcar Silver/Blue; 1999	33	CP
30-7902	Illinois Central Boxcar; includes ProtoFreight Green/Yellow; 1996	85	85
30-7903	New York Central Boxcar; includes ProtoFreight Brown; 1996	85	85
30-7906	Pennsylvania RR Boxcar; includes ProtoFreight Brown; 1996	85	85
30-7907	Union Pacific Boxcar; includes ProtoFreight Brown; 1996	85	85

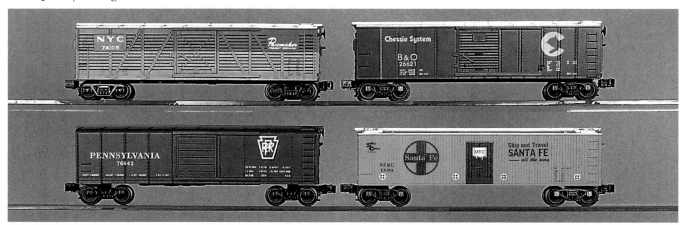

30-7112 New York Central Stock Car 74105, 30-7417 Chessie System Boxcar 26621
30-7418 Pennsylvania Rounded-Roof Boxcar 76642, 30-7808 Santa Fe Reefer 1899

		MSRP	Current
30-7908	Santa Fe Boxcar; includes ProtoFreight Brown; 1996	85	85
30-7909	New York Central Boxcar; includes ProtoFreight Brown; 1996	85	85
30-8401	Pennsylvania RR Die-Cast Boxcar Tuscan Red; 1999	45	CP
30-8402	Western Pacific Die-Cast Boxcar Orange; 1999	45	CP
30-40200	MTH Boxcar w/ sounds Yellow; 1996	N/A	125

Rounded-Roof Boxcars

		MSRP	Current
30-7418	Pennsylvania RR Rounded-Roof Boxcar numbered 76642 Tuscan Red with Keystone herald; 1998	33	33
30-7419	Great Northern Rounded-Roof Boxcar Green with mountain goat graphic; 1998	33	29
30-7429	Baltimore & Ohio Rounded-Roof Boxcar Brown; 1999	33	CP
30-7430	Union Pacific Rounded-Roof Boxcar Yellow/Silver; 1999	33	CP

Refrigerator Cars

		MSRP	Current
30-7800	Pennsylvania RR Reefer numbered 2724 Orange; 1995	28	20

30-7107 Union Pacific Stock Car O.S.L. 48216

		MSRP	Current
30-7801	New York Central Reefer numbered 6078 Orange; 1995	28	28
30-7802	Pacific Fruit Express Reefer numbered 78676 Orange; 1995	28	28
30-7803	Santa Fe Reefer numbered 13448 Orange; 1995	28	25
30-7804	Railway Express Agency Reefer numbered 6435 Orange; 1995	28	28
30-7805	1995 Christmas Reefer numbered 1995 White/Red with wreath graphics lettered "From MTH Electric Trains"; 1995	28	N/A
30-7806	Burlington Reefer numbered BREX 75285 Yellow; 1996	28	28
30-7807	Pacific Fruit Express Reefer numbered 97321 Yellow/Brown lettered "Southern Pacific" and "Union Pacific"; 1996	28	25
30-7808	Santa Fe Reefer numbered 1899 Orange/Silver lettered "Ship and Travel Santa Fe— all the way"; 1996	28	32
30-7809	Pennsylvania RR Reefer numbered 97101 Yellow; 1996	28	33

RailKing Line Wood-Sided Cabooses: top to bottom
30-7701 New York Central Wood-Sided Caboose 18205
30-7721 New York Central Wood-Sided Caboose 19702 (from Sears set)

RailKing Line Wood-Sided Cabooses: left to right
30-7700 Pennsylvania Wood-Sided Caboose 980824
30-7714 Texas & Pacific Wood-Sided Caboose 2569

		MSRP	Current
30-7810	Railway Express Agency Reefer Green; 1996	28	40
30-7811	Amtrak Reefer numbered 1505 Silver; 1997	33	30
30-7812	Florida East Coast Reefer numbered 21019 Red/Gray lettered "Speedway to America's Playground"; 1997	33	33
30-7813	Union Pacific Reefer numbered 73800 Yellow/Silver lettered "Union Pacific Fruit Express"; 1998	33	65
30-7814	Santa Fe Reefer numbered 37625 Red/Black lettered "Shock Control"; 1998	33	30

Stock Cars

		MSRP	Current
30-7100	Pennsylvania RR Stock Car Yellow; 1995	28	28
30-7101	New York Central Stock Car numbered 27641 Yellow; 1995	28	28
30-7102	Union Pacific Stock Car numbered O.S.L. 47729 Yellow lettered "Livestock Dispatch"; 1995	28	28

		MSRP	Current
30-7103	Santa Fe Stock Car numbered 128016 Yellow; 1996	28	25
30-7104	Atlantic Coast Line Stock Car numbered 140297 Yellow; 1995	28	27
30-7105	Union Pacific Stock Car Yellow; 1996	28	26
30-7106	Nickel Plate Stock Car numbered 67534 Tuscan Red; 1996	28	25
30-7107	Union Pacific Stock Car numbered O.S.L. 48216 Yellow/Silver lettered "Livestock Dispatch"; 1996	28	28
30-7108	Santa Fe Stock Car numbered 26425 Red/Silver; 1996	28	28
30-7109	Chicago & North Western Stock Car Green/Yellow; 1996	28	27
30-7110	Denver & Rio Grande Western Stock Car numbered 37713 Orange/Silver; 1997	33	28
30-7111	Erie Stock Car numbered 56634 Black; 1997	33	23
30-7112	New York Central Stock Car numbered 74105 Red/Gray/Silver lettered "Pacemaker Freight Service"; 1998	33	30
30-7113	Chesapeake & Ohio Stock Car numbered 95237 Blue; 1998	33	30
30-7114	Western & Atlantic Stock Car; 19th Century Brown; 1999	33	CP
30-7900	Atlantic Coast Line Stock Car; includes Proto-Freight Yellow; 1996	85	85

RailKing Line Bay Window Cabooses: left to right
30-7712 New York Central Bay Window Caboose 21574
30-7713 Chessie System Bay Window Caboose C-3027

		MSRP	Current
30-7901	Union Pacific Stock Car; includes Proto-Freight Green/Yellow; 1996	85	85
30-7904	New York Central Stock Car; includes Proto-Freight Tuscan Red; 1996	85	85
30-7905	Santa Fe Stock Car; includes Proto-Freight Red; 1996	85	85
30-60080	MTH Stock Car w/ livestock sounds Purple; 1996	N/A	125

Cabooses

Wood-Sided Cabooses

		MSRP	Current
30-7700	Pennsylvania RR Wood-Sided Caboose numbered 980824 Red/Black; 1997	35	36
30-7701	New York Central Wood-Sided Caboose numbered 18205 Red; 1995	35	45
30-7702	Union Pacific Wood-Sided Caboose numbered 3821 Red; 1995	35	30
30-7703	Santa Fe Wood-Sided Caboose numbered 1997 Red; 1995	35	36
30-7704	Norfolk & Western Wood-Sided Caboose numbered 562756 Red; 1995	35	50
30-7705	Nickel Plate Wood-Sided Caboose numbered 1115 Red/White/Black; 1996	35	37
30-7706	Erie Wood-Sided Caboose numbered 04942 Red/Black; 1996	35	35
30-7707	Chicago & North Western Wood-Sided Caboose numbered 12560 Yellow/Green; 1996	35	35

30-7716 Santa Fe Bay Window Caboose 999131

		MSRP	Current
30-7708	Conrail Wood-Sided Caboose numbered CR 22000 Blue; 1996	35	29
30-7709	Chesapeake & Ohio Wood-Sided Caboose numbered 90912 Yellow/Silver lettered "C and O for Progress"; 1997	35	31
30-7710	Union Pacific Wood-Sided Caboose numbered UP 25602 Yellow/Red lettered "Go Big Train"; 1997	35	28
30-7714	Texas & Pacific Wood-Sided Caboose numbered 2569 Red; 1997	40	38
30-7715	Pennsylvania RR Wood-Sided Caboose numbered 980624 Tuscan Red; 1997	40	34
30-7720	Santa Fe Wood-Sided Caboose numbered 1612 Red; 1998	40	30
30-7721	New York Central Wood-Sided Caboose numbered 19702 Tuscan Red; 1998	40	40
30-7722	Pennsylvania RR Wood-Sided Caboose Tuscan Red/Black; 1999	40	CP
30-7723	Baltimore & Ohio Wood-Sided Caboose Red/Black; 1999	40	CP
30-7724	Western & Atlantic Wood-Sided Caboose; 19th Century Brown; 1999	40	CP
30-8501	New York Central Wood-Sided Caboose; Die-Cast; Tuscan Red; 1999	50	CP

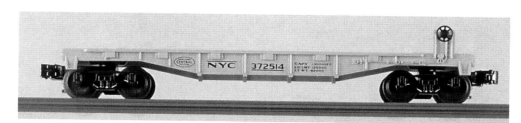

	MSRP	Current
30-8502 Chesapeake & Ohio Wood-Sided Caboose; Die-Cast; Red/Black; 1999	50	CP

Steel Cabooses

	MSRP	Current
30-7727 Chicago North Western Steel Caboose Yellow/Green; 1999	40	CP

Bay Window Cabooses

	MSRP	Current
30-7711 Norfolk Southern Bay Window Caboose Red/Black; 1997	40	31
30-7712 New York Central Bay Window Caboose numbered 21574 Red/Gray; 1997	40	34
30-7713 Chessie System Bay Window Caboose numbered C-3027 Yellow/Silver; 1997	40	31
30-7716 Santa Fe Bay Window Caboose numbered 999131 Silver/Red/Yellow; 1998	40	49
30-7717 Conrail Bay Window Caboose numbered 21146 Blue/Black; 1998	40	41
30-7718 Burlington Northern Santa Fe Bay Window Caboose numbered 12112 Green/Orange; 1998	40	40
30-7719 Fairbanks-Morse Bay Window Caboose numbered 11015 Red/Yellow; 1998	40	35

Work Cabooses

	MSRP	Current
30-7725 Northern Pacific Work Caboose Green; 1999	40	CP
30-7726 New York Central Work Caboose Jade Green; 1999	40	CP

Flatcars and Intermodal Cars

Flatcars

	MSRP	Current
30-7600 Pennsylvania RR Flatcar numbered 468115 Yellow; 1995	23	25
30-7601 New York Central Flatcar numbered 372514 Yellow; 1995	23	25
30-7602 Union Pacific Flatcar numbered 56935 Yellow; 1995	23	27

	MSRP	Current
30-7603 Santa Fe Flatcar numbered 291641 Yellow; 1995	23	30
30-7604 TTUX Flatcar numbered T.T.X. 24071 Yellow lettered "TT Trailer Train"; 1995	23	27
30-7605 Nickel Plate Flatcar Gray; 1996	23	32
30-7606 MTH Construction Company Flatcar numbered 19981 includes one Ertl backhoe; Black; 1996	28	60
30-7607 MTH Classic Auto Transport Flatcar numbered 1952 includes two Blue/White 1952 Cadillacs; Gray; 1996	28	60
30-7608 New York Central Flatcar numbered 499706; includes one Red/Gray "Pacemaker" trailer (6709) Black; 1997	33	28
30-7609 Norfolk Southern Flatcar numbered 60368; includes one White "Triple Crown" trailer; Gray; 1997	33	26
30-7610 MTH Classic Auto Transport Flatcar numbered 1957; includes two Red/White 1957 Chevrolets Black; 1997	33	60
30-7613 MTH Classic Auto Transport Flatcar numbered 1957; includes two Green/Cream 1957 Thunderbirds Black; 1997	33	85
30-7614 MTH Construction Company Flatcar numbered 19971; includes one Ertl dump truck Tuscan Red; 1997	33	29
30-7615 MTH Service Center Flatcar numbered 1955; includes two Green tow trucks Black; 1998	37	45
30-7615 Chessie System Flatcar; includes one Ertl front-end loader/backhoe Blue; 1997	33	N/A

RailKing Line Flatcars: left to right, top to bottom

30-7607 MTH Classic Auto Transport Flatcar w/1952 Cadillacs, 30-7610 MTH Classic Auto Transport Flatcar w/1957 Chevys 30-7608 New York Central Flatcar (w/ "Pacemaker" trailer) 499706, 30-7609 Norfolk Southern Flatcar (w/Triple Crown trailer 60368) 30-76120 MTH Construction Flatcar (w/road grader) 19983

		MSRP	Current
30-7616	MTH Construction Company Flatcar numbered 19981; includes one Ertl earth mover Gray; 1998	33	80
30-7617	MTH Flatcar Black; 1998	37	45
30-7619	MTH Construction Company Flatcar numbered 19984; includes one Ertl front-end loader/backhoe Gray; 1997	33	40
30-7620	MTH Construction Company Flatcar; includes one Ertl road grader Gray; 1998	33	40
30-7621	MTH Transport Company Flatcar numbered 1959; includes one Red/White airplane (400E) Black; 1998	37	40
30-7623	MTH Classic Auto Transport Flatcar; includes two Ertl fire cars Gray; 1998	37	60
30-7624	MTH Classic Auto Transport Flatcar numbered 1964; includes two Red/White Ertl1964 Corvettes Black; 1998	37	37
30-7625	MTH Classic Auto Transport Flatcar; includes two Ertl 1959 Checker cabs Black; 1998	37	37
30-7626	Pennsylvania RR Flatcar numbered 474399; includes one Tuscan Red "TrucTrain" trailer (PRR15104) Black; 1998	33	35

		MSRP	Current
30-7627	Florida East Coast Flatcar numbered 64273; includes one Red "Speedway to America's Playground" trailer Black; 1998	33	35
30-7629	MTH Transport Company Flatcar numbered 1979; includes one Ertl fire truck Gray; 1998	33	39
30-7631	MTH Service Center Flatcar; includes two Ertl 1955 wreckers Black; 1998	37	40
30-7632	Union Pacific Flatcar; includes one Silver "Trailer Service" trailer Brown; 1999	33	CP
30-7633	Baltimore & Ohio Flatcar; includes one Yellow/Red "Trailer Freight Service" trailer Black; 1999	33	CP
30-7634	MTH Classic Auto Transport Flatcar numbered 1969; includes two Blue Ertl 1969 Camaros Black; 1999	37	CP
30-7635	Western & Atlantic Flatcar; 19th Century Brown; 1999	33	CP
30-7636	Southern Pacific Bulkhead Flatcar; includes cut lumber load Brown; 1999	30	CP
30-7637	Erie-Lackawanna Bulkhead Flatcar; includes cut lumber load Black; 1999	30	CP

30-7622 New York Central Depressed-Center Flatcar (w/Blue New Holland front-end loader) 21136

		MSRP	Current
30-7639	MTH Transport Company Flatcar; includes two Ertl 1968 GTOs Black; 1999	40	CP
30-7640	Union 76 Center Flatcar; includes two Ertl 1955 Union 76 wreckers Black; 1999	40	CP
30-7642	MTH Farm Equipment Flatcar; includes two Ertl tractors Black; 1999	40	CP
30-7647	MTH Transport Company Flatcar; includes two Ertl 1950 panel trucks Gray; 1999	40	CP
30-7648	Western Maryland Operating Flatcar; includes log load Brown; 1999	40	CP
30-7649	Northern Pacific Operating Flatcar; includes log load Black; 1999	40	CP
30-7658	MTH Transport Operating Flatcar; includes one operating helicopter Gray; 1999	60	CP
30-8303	Milwaukee Road Die-Cast Flatcar; includes two Ertl 1932 panel trucks Brown; 1999	50	CP
30-8304	Chesapeake & Ohio Die-Cast Flatcar; includes two Ertl 1932 panel trucks Black; 1999	50	CP
30-76120	MTH Construction Company Flatcar numbered 19983; includes one Yellow road grader Gray; 1998	33	33

Depressed-Center Flatcars

		MSRP	Current
30-7611	MTH Depressed-Center Flatcar; includes one Blue tractor Gray; 1997	33	29

		MSRP	Current
30-7612	MTH Depressed-Center Flatcar; includes transformer load Red; 1999	33	CP
30-7618	MTH Depressed-Center Flatcar; includes one Ertl bulldozer Gray; 1998	33	40
30-7622	MTH Depressed-Center Flatcar numbered 21136; includes one Blue New Holland front-end loader Black; 1998	60	30
30-8301	Santa Fe Die-Cast Depressed-Center Flatcar; includes transformer load Red; 1999	45	CP
30-8302	Illinois Central Die-Cast Depressed-Center Flatcar includes transformer load Brown; 1999	45	CP

Automobile Carrier

		MSRP	Current
30-7628	MTH Auto Transportation Auto Carrier Flatcar; includes two Ertl 1949 Ford coupes and two Ertl 1952 Cadillacs Brown; 1998	55	55
30-7638	MTH Auto Transportation Auto Carrier Flatcar; includes two Ertl 1967 Pontiac Firebirds and two Ertl 1970 Chevy Novas Brown; 1999	40	CP
30-7656	MTH Auto Transportation Auto Carrier Flatcar; includes four Ertl 1957 Chevys Gray; 1999	40	CP

Intermodal Well Cars

		MSRP	Current
30-7643	Hanjin Husky Stack Car; includes two White containers Yellow; 1999	40	CP
30-7644	Santa Fe Husky Stack Car; includes two Blue containers Red; 1999	40	CP

Gondolas

		MSRP	Current
30-7200	Pennsylvania RR Gondola numbered 367829 Green; 1995	26	55

RailKing Line Gondolas: left to right
30-7209 Pennsylvania RR Gondola (w/crates) 376901
30-7211 CSX Gondola (w/crates) 11671

		MSRP	Current
30-7201	New York Central Gondola numbered 762453 Green; 1995	26	26
30-7202	Union Pacific Gondola Green; 1995	26	26
30-7203	Santa Fe Gondola numbered 166593 Green; 1995	26	25
30-7204	Milwaukee Road Gondola numbered 93077; includes three crates Green; 1995	26	26
30-7205	Chicago & North Western Gondola; includes three crates Yellow; 1996	26	26
30-7206	Norfolk & Western Gondola; includes three crates Brown; 1996	26	26
30-7207	Conrail Gondola; includes three crates Gray; 1996	26	26
30-7208	Union Pacific Gondola numbered 65239; includes three Tan crates Tuscan Red; 1997	30	23
30-7209	Pennsylvania RR Gondola numbered 376901; includes three White crates Black; 1997	30	25
30-7209	Pennsylvania RR Gondola numbered 376829; includes three Tan crates Black; 1997	N/A	N/A
30-7210	Northern Pacific Gondola; includes three crates Green; 1997	30	30
30-7211	CSX Gondola numbered 11671; includes three Tan crates Black; 1997	30	30

		MSRP	Current
30-7212	Pennsylvania RR Gondola; includes three crates Black; 1997	30	30
30-7213	Baltimore & Ohio Gondola numbered XM890 Black; 1998	30	30
30-7214	Chesapeake & Ohio Gondola numbered 31722 Black; 1998	30	30
30-7215	Nickel Plate Gondola; includes junk load Black; 1999	30	CP
30-8201	Union Pacific Die-Cast Gondola Car; includes junk load Brown; 1999	45	CP
30-8202	Boston & Maine Die-Cast Gondola Car; includes junk load Blue; 1999	45	CP

Hopper Cars

Ore Cars
		MSRP	Current
30-7518	Baltimore & Ohio Ore Car numbered 6453 Gray; 1998	30	30
30-7519	Chicago & North Western Ore Car numbered 55378 Green; 1998	30	30
30-7522	Pennsylvania RR Ore Car; includes ore load Tuscan Red; 1999	33	CP
30-7527	Union Pacific Ore Car; includes ore load Silver; 1999	33	CP

4-Bay Hopper Cars
		MSRP	Current
30-7500	Pennsylvania RR Hopper Car Black; 1995	28	39
30-7501	New York Central Hopper Car numbered 868001 Black; 1995	28	25
30-7502	Union Pacific Hopper Car numbered 91084 Black; 1995	28	28
30-7503	Santa Fe Hopper Car numbered 181764 Black; 1995	28	60

30-7501 New York Central 4-Bay Hopper 868001

		MSRP	Current
30-7504	Burlington Hopper Car numbered 190359 Black; 1995	28	30
30-7505	Nickel Plate Road Hopper Car numbered 30160 Black; 1996	28	24
30-7506	Norfolk & Western Hopper Car numbered 131248 Black; 1996	28	28
30-7507	Chesapeake & Ohio Hopper Car numbered 69576 Black; 1996	28	28
30-7508	Pennsylvania RR Hopper Car numbered 192164 Tuscan Red; 1997	30	24
30-7509	Union Pacific Hopper Car numbered 12727 Gray; 1997	30	25
30-7510	Norfolk Southern Hopper Car Gray; 1997	33	33
30-7511	Chicago & North Western Hopper Car numbered 67655 Green; 1997	33	25
30-7512	Northern Pacific Hopper Car numbered 70245 Black; 1997	33	30
30-7513	New York Central Hopper Car numbered 904420 Black; 1997	33	24
30-7514	Chessie System Hopper Car numbered 82701 Black; 1997	33	26

		MSRP	Current
30-7515	Norfolk & Western Hopper Car numbered 30771 Gray; 1998	33	33
30-7516	Western Maryland Hopper Car numbered 90005 Tuscan Red; 1998	33	33
30-7517	New York Central Hopper Car numbered 831916 Black; 1998	33	33
30-7523	Erie-Lackawanna Hopper Car; includes coal load Black; 1999	33	CP
30-7524	Southern Hopper Car; includes coal load Brown; 1999	33	CP
30-7525	Norfolk & Western Hopper Car; includes coal load Black; 1999	40	CP
30-8001	Baltimore & Ohio Die-Cast Hopper Car; includes coal load Black; 1999	45	CP
30-8002	Lehigh Valley Die-Cast Hopper Car; includes coal load White; 1999	45	CP

Dump Cars

		MSRP	Current
30-7924	Northern Pacific Dump Car Black; 1999	40	CP
30-7925	CSX Dump Car Gray; 1999	40	CP

RailKing Line 4-Bay Hoppers: left to right
30-7505 Nickel Plate Road 4-Bay Hopper 30160
30-7512 Northern Pacific 4-Bay Hopper 70245

RailKing Line Single-Dome Tank Car: left to right
30-7310 New York Central Tank Car 5791
30-7303 Santa Fe Tank Car 100943

Tank Cars

		MSRP	Current

Single-Dome Tank Cars

		MSRP	Current
30-7300	Pennsylvania RR Tank Car numbered 498639 Silver; 1995	28	31
30-7301	New York Central Tank Car numbered 4725 Silver; 1995	28	28
30-7302	Union Pacific Tank Car numbered 70084 Silver; 1995	28	30
30-7303	Santa Fe Tank Car numbered 100943 Silver; 1995	28	28
30-7304	Baltimore & Ohio Tank Car numbered X416 Silver; 1995	28	28
30-7305	Conrail Tank Car numbered 5010 Blue; 1996	28	28
30-7306	Santa Fe Tank Car numbered 100943 Red lettered "Shock Control"; 1996	28	35
30-7307	Chicago & North Western Tank Car numbered 32308 Green; 1996	28	30
30-7308	Chesapeake & Ohio Tank Car numbered 4123 Yellow; 1997	30	30
30-7309	Union Pacific Tank Car numbered 69012 Black; 1997	30	24
30-7310	New York Central Tank Car numbered 5791 Black/Silver; 1997	33	26
30-7311	Sinclair Tank Car Green; 1997	33	45
30-7312	Norfolk Southern Tank Car numbered 10238 Black; 1997	33	26

		MSRP	Current
30-7314	Esso Tank Car Blue; 1998	33	33
30-7315	Denver & Rio Grande Western Tank Car Orange/Silver; 1998	33	30
30-7316	Texaco Tank Car numbered 878991 White; 1999	33	CP
30-7317	Pennsylvania RR Tank Car numbered 500001 White/Tuscan Red; 1999	33	CP
30-8101	Shell Die-Cast Tank Car Black; 1999	45	CP
30-8102	Denver Rio Grande Die-Cast Tank Car Orange; 1999	45	CP

3-Dome Tank Cars

30-7318	Union Pacific 3-Dome Tank Car Black; 1999	33	CP
30-7319	Pennsylvania RR 3-Dome Tank Car Silver; 1999	33	CP

Work Cars

Bunk Cars

30-7216	Amtrak Bunk Car Orange; 1999	30	CP
30-7920	Conrail Bunk Car Orange; 1999	40	CP

Crane Cars

30-7910	Pennsylvania RR Crane Car N/A; 1997	50	50
30-7911	New York Central Crane Car numbered X-27 Black/Silver; 1997	50	50
30-7916	Chessie System Crane Car numbered 900029 Blue/Yellow/Orange; 1998	50	50
30-7917	Conrail Crane Car numbered X47 Orange/Black; 1998	50	50

30-7911 New York Central Crane X-27
30-7912 New York Central Crane Tender X-27

30-7917 Operating Crane Car Conrail X47

		MSRP	Current
30-7918	Amtrak Crane Car Orange; 1999	50	CP
30-7919	Nickel Plate Crane Car Black; 1999	50	CP
30-7928	MTH Crane Car Gray/Black; 1999	50	CP

Crane Tenders

		MSRP	Current
30-7912	New York Central Wood-Sided Crane Tender Car numbered X-27 Black/Silver; 1998	40	35
30-7913	Northern Pacific Wood-Sided Crane Tender Car Green; 1998	40	35

Searchlight Cars

		MSRP	Current
30-7914	New York Central Searchlight Car Black; 1996	40	35
30-7915	Union Pacific Searchlight Car Brown; 1998	40	35
30-7926	Conrail Searchlight Car Gray; 1999	40	CP
30-7927	Amtrak Searchlight Car Black; 1999	40	CP

		MSRP	Current
Mixed Sets			
30-7001	Wabash 6-Car Freight Set Various; 1999	200	CP
30-7002	Southern 6-Car Freight Set Various; 1999	200	CP
30-7003	Central RR of New Jersey 6-Car Freight Set; includes no. 22861 rounded-roof boxcar, 90170 gondola with junk load, 6 crane car, 92615 crane tender, 92511 single-dome tank car, 91515 bay window caboose Various; 1999	200	CP
30-7004	6-Car Freight Set Various; 1999	200	CP
30-7005	Union Pacific 6-Car Freight Set; includes modern reefer, Husky Stack, Ps-2 discharge hopper, 4-bay ribbed hopper, 33K tank car, steel caboose Various; 1999	200	CP
30-7006	Great Northern 6-Car Freight Set; includes boxcar, hopper car, gondola, crane, crane tender, steel caboose Various; 1999	200	CP
30-7520	Chesapeake & Ohio 4-Bay Hopper 6-Car Set Various; 1999	180	CP
30-7521	Union Pacific 4-Bay Hopper 6-Car Set Various; 1999	180	CP
65808134022	Sears 3-Car Set; includes New York Central 2-6-0 Mogul numbered 2743; 30-76120 MTH Construction Company flatcar 19983; 30-N/A Timken Roller Bearing boxcar (exclusive to Sears Set) 60368 TRB; 30-7721 New York Central wood-sided caboose 19702 Various; 1998	N/A	N/A

RailKing Line
Passenger Cars

RailKing passenger cars match the look of their category-counterpart motive power. From heavy-weight "Madison-style" cars (coaches, combines, diners, baggage cars, observation cars) in drab Pullman Green through colorful smooth-sided cars from the streamlined era, to the latest hi-level Amtrak coaches and Metroliner "Heritage Fleet" cars, MTH RailKing passenger cars cover the field. The carbodies are made of ABS, the trucks are die-cast (as are the operating couplers), the interiors are lighted, and the decoration is crisp. Some cars also have detailed interiors. Though they'll never be mistaken for "scale" models, RailKing passenger cars have that toy train look without looking undersized or misproportioned.

Number 30-6501 Two-Car Superliner Set with Sleeping Car 32013 and Dining Car 38026

RailKing Line Overton-Style Passenger Coaches: left to right, top to bottom
30-6400 Western & Atlantic RR 3-Car Overton Passenger Coach Set 8, 12, 16
30-6404 Western & Atlantic RR 4-Car Overton Passenger Coach Set 20, 22, 24, 28

		MSRP	Current

Overton

		MSRP	Current
30-6400	Western & Atlantic RR 3-Car Overton Passenger Coach Set; includes cars numbered 8, 12, and 16 Yellow/Brown; 1997	119	139
30-6404	Western & Atlantic RR 4-Car Overton Passenger Coach Set; includes cars numbered 20, 22, 24, and 28 Olive Drab/Black; 1998	160	175

Madison

4-Car Sets

		MSRP	Current
30-6230	Denver & Rio Grande Western 4-Car O27 Madison Passenger Set; includes baggage car no. 711, coach 1013, coach 1011, and observation "Granite Canyon" Silver/Orange; 1997	159	169
30-6240	Southern 4-Car O27 Madison Passenger Set Two-tone Green; 1997	159	190

		MSRP	Current
30-6244	Nickel Plate 4-Car O27 Madison Passenger Set Pullman Green; 1998	160	130
30-6248	Chesapeake & Ohio 4-Car O27 Madison Passenger Set Blue/Yellow/Gray; 1998	160	125
30-6250	Pennsylvania RR 4-Car O27 Madison Passenger Set Tuscan Red; 1998	160	125
30-6252	Union Pacific 4-Car O27 Madison Passenger Set Yellow/Gray; 1998	160	135
30-6256	New York Central 4-Car O27 Madison Passenger Set; includes baggage car no. 8986, coach "Wappingers Falls," coach "Park Trail," and observation "Maumee River" Two-tone Gray/Black; 1998	160	150
30-6258	Central RR of New Jersey 4-Car O27 Madison Passenger Set; includes baggage car no. 210 coach 913, coach 918, and observation "Monmouth" Pullman Green/Black; 1999	160	CP

		MSRP	Current
30-6260	Reading 4-Car O27 Madison Passenger Set; includes baggage car no. 1715, coach 1505, coach 1509, and observation 10 Dark Green/Black; 1999	160	CP
30-6262	Wabash 4-Car O27 Madison Passenger Set Dark Blue; 1999	80	CP
30-6264	New York Central 4-Car O27 Madison Passenger Set Pullman Green; 1999	160	CP

2-Car Sets

		MSRP	Current
30-6204	Pennsylvania RR 2-Car O27 Madison Combo/Diner Set Tuscan Red; 1997	80	80
30-6214	New York Central 2-Car O27 Madison Combo/Diner Set Pullman Green; 1997	80	80
30-6224	Texas & Pacific 2-Car O27 Madison Combo/Diner Set; includes combine no. 800 and diner 1015 Blue/Gray; 1997	80	80
30-6234	Denver & Rio Grande Western 2-Car O27 Madison Combo/Diner Set Orange/Silver; 1997	80	80
30-6241	Southern 2-Car O27 Madison Combo/Diner Set Two-tone Green; 1998	80	100
30-6245	Nickel Plate 2-Car O27 Madison Combo/Diner Set Pullman Green; 1998	80	295

RailKing Line Madison-Style O27 Passenger Sets/Cars: left to right, top to bottom
30-6240 Southern *Crescent Limited* Railway Express Agency Car 0200, 30-6249 Chesapeake & Ohio Combine 50
30-6250 Pennsylvania RR Coach 4363, 30-6249 Chesapeake & Ohio Diner 10
30-6240 Southern *Crescent Limited* Pullman "Henry W. Grady," 30-6250 Pennsylvania RR Observation Car 6905

		MSRP	Current
30-6249	Chesapeake & Ohio 2-Car O27 Madison Combo/Diner Set; includes combine no. 50 and diner 10 Blue/Yellow/Gray; 1998	80	80
30-6253	Union Pacific 2-Car O27 Madison Combo/Diner Set Yellow/Gray; 1998	80	75
30-6257	New York Central 2-Car O27 Madison Combo/Diner Set Two-tone Gray Painted; 1998	80	75
30-6263	Wabash 2-Car O27 Madison Combo/Diner Set Blue; 1999	80	CP

Baggage Cars

		MSRP	Current
30-6200	Pennsylvania RR O27 Madison Baggage Car Tuscan Red; 1997	35	40
30-6210	New York Central O27 Madison Baggage Car Pullman Green; 1997	35	40
30-6220	Texas & Pacific O27 Madison Baggage Car numbered 910 Blue/Gray; 1997	35	40

Coach Cars

		MSRP	Current
30-6201	Pennsylvania RR O27 Madison Coach Car Tuscan Red; 1997	35	40

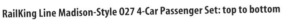

RailKing Line Madison-Style O27 4-Car Passenger Set: top to bottom
30-6256 New York Central Baggage Car 8986
         New York Central Coach "Park Trail"
         New York Central Coach "Wappingers Falls"
         New York Central Observation Car "Maumee River"

		MSRP	Current
30-6202	Pennsylvania RR O27 Madison Coach Car Tuscan Red; 1997	**35**	**40**
30-6211	New York Central O27 Madison Coach Car Pullman Green; 1997	**35**	**35**
30-6212	New York Central O27 Madison Coach Car Pullman Green; 1997	**35**	**35**
30-6221	Texas & Pacific O27 Madison Coach Car numbered 1307 Blue/Gray; 1997	**35**	**40**
30-6222	Texas & Pacific O27 Madison Coach Car numbered 1302 Blue/Gray; 1997	**35**	**40**
30-6231	Denver & Rio Grande Western O27 Madison Coach Car Orange/Silver; 1997	**40**	**40**

RailKing Line Madison-Style O27 4-Car Passenger Set: top to bottom
30-6258 Jersey Central Lines Baggage Car 210
         Jersey Central Lines Coach 913
         Jersey Central Lines Coach 918
         Jersey Central Lines Observation Car "Monmouth"

		MSRP	Current

Observation Cars

		MSRP	Current
30-6203	Pennsylvania RR O27 Madison Observation Car Tuscan Red; 1997	**35**	**40**
30-6213	New York Central O27 Madison Observation Car Pullman Green; 1997	**35**	**35**
30-6223	Texas & Pacific O27 Madison Observation Car Blue/Gray; 1997	**35**	**40**

Streamlined

4-Car Sets

		MSRP	Current
30-6060	Southern Pacific 4-Car O27 Streamlined Passenger Set Orange/Red; 1997	**159**	**250**

		MSRP	Current
30-6070	Pennsylvania RR 4-Car O27 Streamlined Passenger Set Aluminum/Black; 1997	159	180
30-6080	New York Central 4-Car O27 Streamlined Passenger Set Two-tone Gray; 1997	159	160
30-6090	Milwaukee Road 4-Car O27 Streamlined Passenger Set Orange/Maroon painted; 1998	160	250
30-6094	Denver & Rio Grande Western 4-Car O27 Streamlined Passenger Set Silver/Yellow painted; 1998	160	160
30-6098	Delaware & Hudson 4-Car O27 Streamlined Passenger Set Silver/Yellow/Blue painted; 1998	160	160
30-6103	Santa Fe 4-Car O27 Streamlined Passenger Set Silver/Red/Yellow; 1998	160	160
30-6104	Pennsylvania RR 4-Car O27 Streamlined Passenger Set Red/Tuscan Red/Black; 1998	160	160
30-6107	Union Pacific 4-Car O27 Streamlined Passenger Set Yellow/Gray; 1998	160	160
30-6109	Southern Pacific 4-Car O27 Streamlined Passenger Set Orange/Red; 1999	160	160
30-6110	New York Central 4-Car O27 Streamlined Passenger Set Two-tone Gray; 1999	160	CP

RailKing Line Streamlined O27 Passenger Car Sets/Cars: left to right, top to bottom

30-6094 Denver & Rio Grande Western Baggage Car 763, 30-6063 Southern Pacific Combine 6099

30-6070 Pennsylvania Coach 4008, 30-6063 Southern Pacific Diner 10214

30-6094 Denver & Rio Grande Western Vista Dome 5200, 30-6090 Milwaukee Road Observation Car "Miller"

		MSRP	Current
30-6111	Baltimore & Ohio 4-Car O27 Streamlined Passenger Set; includes baggage car no. 662, coach 3567, vista dome 5551, and observation 7512 Blue/Gray; 1999	160	CP
30-6112	Electro-Motive Division 4-Car O27 Streamlined Passenger Set Blue/Silver/Black; 1999	160	CP
30-6113	New York Central Empire State Express 4-Car O27 Streamlined Passenger Set Aluminum; 1999	160	CP
30-6120	Santa Fe 4-Car O27 Streamlined Passenger Set Silver/Red/Yellow; 1999	160	CP
30-6123	Southern 4-Car O27 Streamlined Passenger Set Green/White; 1999	160	CP
30-6131	New Haven 4-Car O27 Streamlined Passenger Set Silver/Orange; 1999	160	CP
30-6133	Reading 4-Car O27 Streamlined Passenger Set Aluminum; 1999	160	CP

RailKing Line Streamlined Passenger Cars: top to bottom

30-6050 Burlington Streamlined O27
California Zephyr Baggage Car 900

30-6051 Burlington Streamlined O27
California Zephyr Coach 4707

30-6052 Burlington Streamlined O27
California Zephyr Vista Dome 4723

30-6053 Burlington Streamlined O27
California Zephyr Observation Car 302

		MSRP	Current
30-6135	New York Central 4-Car O27 Streamlined Passenger Set Two-tone Gray; 1999	**160**	**CP**

2-Car Sets

		MSRP	Current
30-6004	Amtrak 2-Car O27 Streamlined Combo/Diner Set Silver/Red/White/Blue painted; 1997	**80**	**70**
30-6014	Santa Fe 2-Car O27 Streamlined Combo/Diner Set Silver/Red; 1997	**80**	**70**
30-6024	New York Central 2-Car O27 Streamlined Combo/Diner Set Two-tone Gray; 1997	**80**	**80**

		MSRP	Current
30-6034	Union Pacific 2-Car O27 Streamlined Combo/Diner Set Yellow/Gray painted; 1997	**80**	**80**
30-6044	Florida East Coast 2-Car O27 Streamlined Combo/Diner Set Red/Yellow painted; 1998	**80**	**90**
30-6054	Burlington 2-Car O27 *California Zephyr* Streamlined Combo/Diner Set Aluminum painted; 1998	**80**	**100**
30-6063	Southern Pacific 2-Car O27 Streamlined Combo/Diner Set numbered 6099 and 10214 Red/Orange painted; 1998	**80**	**100**

		MSRP	Current
30-6064	Southern Pacific 2-Car O27 Streamlined Combo/Diner Set Red/Orange; 1999	80	CP
30-6073	Pennsylvania RR 2-Car O27 Streamlined Combo/Diner Set Silver/Black painted; 1998	80	90
30-6083	New York Central 2-Car O27 Streamlined Combo/Diner Set Two-tone Gray painted; 1998	80	80
30-6084	New York Central Lightning 2-Car O27 Streamlined Combo/Diner Set Two-tone Gray; 1998	80	CP
30-6091	Milwaukee Road 2-Car O27 Streamlined Combo/Diner Set; Orange/Maroon painted; 1998	80	100
30-6095	Denver & Rio Grande Western 2-Car O27 Streamlined Combo/Diner Set Silver/Orange painted; 1998	80	80
30-6099	Delaware & Hudson 2-Car O27 Streamlined Combo/Diner Set Silver/Yellow/Blue painted; 1998	80	80
30-6105	Santa Fe 2-Car O27 Streamlined Combo/Diner Set Silver/Red/Yellow painted; 1998	80	75
30-6106	Pennsylvania RR 2-Car O27 Streamlined Combo/Diner Set; includes combine no. 5109 and diner 4518 Tuscan Red painted; 1998	80	75
30-6108	Union Pacific 2-Car O27 Streamlined Combo/Diner Set Yellow/Red/Black painted; 1999	80	80
30-6126	New York Central *Empire State Express* 2-Car O27 Streamlined Combo/Diner Set Aluminum; 1999	80	CP
30-6127	Baltimore & Ohio 2-Car O27 Streamlined Combo/Diner Set Blue/White/Black; 1999	80	CP
30-6128	Electro-Motive Division 2-Car O27 Streamlined Combo/Diner Set Blue/Silver/Black; 1999	80	CP
30-6129	Santa Fe 2-Car O27 Streamlined Combo/Diner Set Silver/Red/Yellow; 1999	80	CP
30-6130	Southern 2-Car O27 Streamlined Combo/Diner Set Green/White; 1999	80	CP

Baggage Cars

		MSRP	Current
30-6000	Amtrak O27 Streamlined Baggage Car Silver/Red/White/Blue lettered "New York 'Railway Express'"; 1996	40	40
30-6010	Santa Fe O27 Streamlined Baggage Car Silver/Red; 1996	40	40
30-6020	New York Central O27 Streamlined Baggage Car numbered 9152 Gray; 1997	35	75
30-6030	Union Pacific O27 Streamlined Baggage Car Yellow/Gray; 1997	35	45
30-6040*	Florida East Coast O27 Streamlined Baggage Car numbered 443. *Reviewed in CTT September 1997* Red/Yellow; 1997	35	49
30-6050	Burlington O27 *California Zephyr* Streamlined Baggage Car numbered 900 Aluminum lettered "Railway Express"; 1997	35	50

Coach Cars

		MSRP	Current
30-6001	Amtrak O27 Streamlined Coach Car Silver/Red/White/Blue; 1996	40	40
30-6002	Amtrak O27 Streamlined Coach Car Silver/Red/White/Blue; 1996	40	40
30-6011	Santa Fe O27 Streamlined Coach Car Silver/Red; 1996	40	40
30-6021	New York Central O27 Streamlined Coach Car numbered 10510 Gray; 1997	35	75
30-6031	Union Pacific O27 Streamlined Coach Car Yellow/Gray; 1997	35	35
30-6041*	Florida East Coast O27 Streamlined Coach Car numbered 2629. *Reviewed in CTT September 1997* Red/Yellow; 1997	35	49
30-6051	Burlington O27 *California Zephyr* Streamlined Coach Car numbered 4707 Aluminum; 1997	35	50
30-6061	Southern Pacific O27 Streamlined Coach Car Red/Orange; 1997	40	60
30-6071	Pennsylvania RR O27 Streamlined Coach Car Silver; 1997	40	55

**RailKing Line Amtrak Genesis
Passenger Set (w/o locomotive) and
Add-On 2-Car Sleeper/Diner Set: top to
bottom**

30-4018 Amtrak Locomotive (shown in
RailKing Diesel Locomotives chapter)

      Amtrak Coach Baggage 31019

      Amtrak Coach 34022

      Amtrak Coach 34077

      Amtrak Lounge Cafe 33010

30-6501 Amtrak Sleeping Car 32013

      Amtrak Dining Car 38026

		MSRP	Current			MSRP	Current
30-6081	New York Central O27 Streamlined Coach Car Two-tone Gray; 1997	**40**	**40**	**30-6116**	Baltimore & Ohio O27 Streamlined Coach Car Blue/White/Black; 1999	**40**	**CP**
30-6102	Santa Fe O27 Streamlined Coach Car numbered 3161 Silver/Red/Yellow; 1998	**40**	**40**	**30-6117**	Electro-Motive Division O27 Streamlined Coach Car Blue/Silver/Black; 1999	**40**	**CP**
30-6114	Southern Pacific O27 Streamlined Coach Car Red/Orange; 1999	**40**	**CP**	**30-6119**	New York Central *Empire State Express* O27 Streamlined Coach Car Aluminum; 1999	**40**	**CP**
30-6115	New York Central O27 Streamlined Coach Car numbered 2666 Two-tone Gray; 1999	**40**	**CP**	**30-6124**	Southern O27 Streamlined Coach Car Green/White; 1999	**40**	**CP**

	MSRP	Current
30-6132 New Haven O27 Streamlined Coach Car Silver/Orange; 1999	40	CP
30-6134 Reading O27 Streamlined Coach Car Aluminum; 1999	40	CP

Observation Cars

	MSRP	Current
30-6003 Amtrak O27 Streamlined Observation Car Silver/Red/White/Blue; 1996	40	40
30-6013 Santa Fe O27 Streamlined Observation Car Silver/Red; 1996	40	40
30-6023 New York Central O27 Streamlined Observation Car numbered 10633 Gray; 1997	35	75
30-6033 Union Pacific O27 Streamlined Observation Car Yellow/Gray; 1997	35	45
30-6043* Florida East Coast O27 Streamlined Observation Car numbered 3300. *Reviewed in CTT September 1997* Red/Yellow; 1997	35	49
30-6053 Burlington O27 *California Zephyr* Streamlined Observation Car numbered 302 Aluminum; 1997	35	50

Vista Domes

	MSRP	Current
30-6012 Santa Fe O27 Streamlined Vista Dome Car Silver/Red; 1996	40	40
30-6022 New York Central O27 Streamlined Vista Dome Car Two-tone Gray; 1997	35	75
30-6032 Union Pacific O27 Streamlined Vista Dome Car Yellow/Gray; 1997	35	45
30-6042* Florida East Coast O27 Streamlined Vista Dome Car numbered 3012. *Reviewed in CTT September 1997* Red/Yellow; 1997	35	49

	MSRP	Current
30-6052 Burlington O27 *California Zephyr* Streamlined Vista Dome Car numbered 4723 Aluminum; 1997	35	50
30-6062 Southern Pacific O27 Streamlined Vista Dome Car Red/Orange; 1997	40	60
30-6072 Pennsylvania RR O27 Streamlined Vista Dome Car Silver; 1997	40	50
30-6082 New York Central O27 Streamlined Vista Dome Car Two-tone Gray; 1997	40	40
30-6118 Southern Pacific O27 Streamlined Vista Dome Car Red/Orange; 1999	40	CP
30-6121 Santa Fe O27 Streamlined Vista Dome Car Silver/Red/Yellow; 1999	40	CP

Superliner

4-Car Sets

	MSRP	Current
30-6500* Amtrak 4-Car O27 SuperLiner Set (from no. 30-4018 Amtrak Genesis set); includes coach/baggage car no. 31019, coach 34022, coach 34077, and lounge/cafe 33010. *Reviewed in CTT February 1999* 3 stripes; Silver/Red/White/Blue; 1999	180	CP

2-Car Sets

	MSRP	Current
30-6501 Amtrak 2-Car O27 SuperLiner Sleeper/Diner Set; includes sleeping car no. 32013 and diner 38026 3 stripes; Silver/Red/White/Blue; 1998	80	80

Transitional Sleeper Cars

	MSRP	Current
30-6503 Amtrak SuperLiner Transitional Sleeper Car 3 stripes; Silver/Red/White/Blue; 1999	50	CP

Tinplate Traditions Line
Locomotives, Rolling Stock, and Passenger Cars

Tinplate Traditions has to be Mike Wolf's favorite. These reproductions (mostly) of Lionel Standard gauge (and some O) beauties are the trains that started it all, going back to when Mike worked for Jerry Williams at Williams Reproductions. Included here are the MTH steam engines, electric locomotives, freight cars, and passenger cars produced since 1993. Locomotive listings include Traditional (Bild-a-Loco-type motor and mechanical e-unit) and Contemporary (Pittman motor, electronic e-unit). Trim varies (i.e., nickel or brass).

Number 10-1022 408E Stephen Girard Electric Locomotive

10-1062 263E (Columbia 2-4-2) Steam Locomotive and Tender (Blue)
10-1063 263E (Columbia 2-4-2) Steam Locomotive and Tender (Gray)

	MSRP	Current

Steam Locomotives

Columbia (2-4-2)

10–1062	263E Steam Locomotive and Tender Blue; 1998		
	(–0) O gauge with Traditional features	400	450
	(–1) O gauge with Contemporary features	400	450
10–1063	263E Steam Locomotive and Tender Gray/Nickel; 1998		
	(–0) O gauge with Traditional features	400	400
	(–1) O gauge with Contemporary features	400	400
10–3001	260E Steam Locomotive and Tender Black; 1999		
	(–0) O gauge with Traditional features	400	CP
	(–1) O gauge with Contemporary features	30	CP
10–3002	260E Steam Locomotive and Tender Black; 1999		
	(–0) O gauge with Traditional features	400	CP
	(–1) O gauge with Contemporary features	430	CP

	MSRP	Current

Atlantic (4-4-2)

10–1091	392E Pennsylvania RR Steam Locomotive and Tender Gray; 1998		
	(–0) Standard gauge with Traditional features	700	700
	(–1) Standard gauge with Contemporary features	700	700
10–1092	392E Pennsylvania RR Steam Locomotive and Tender Black; 1998		
	(–0) Standard gauge with Traditional features	700	700
	(–1) Standard gauge with Contemporary features	700	700

Jubilee (4-4-4)

10–1058	400E New York Central Steam Locomotive and Tender Gray; 1997		
	(–) Standard gauge with Contemporary features	800	800
10–1059	400E New York Central Steam Locomotive and Tender Gray; 1997		
	(–) Standard gauge with Traditional features	800	800
10–1060	400E New York Central Steam Locomotive and Tender Black; 1997		
	(–) Standard gauge with Contemporary features	800	950

10-1091 392E (Atlantic 4-4-2) Pennsylvania Steam Locomotive and Tender (Gray)
10-1092 392E (Atlantic 4-4-2) Pennsylvania Steam Locomotive and Tender (Black)

10-1058 400E (Jubilee 4-4-4) New York Central Steam Locomotive and Tender (Gray)
10-1060 400E (Jubilee 4-4-4) New York Central Steam Locomotive and Tender (Black)

		MSRP	Current
10–1061*	400E New York Central Steam Locomotive and Tender. *Reviewed in CTT November 1998* Black; 1997		
	(**–**) Standard gauge with Traditional features	800	850
10–1112	400E Steam Locomotive and Tender Blue; 1999		
	(**–0**) Standard gauge with Traditional features	800	CP
	(**–1**) Standard gauge with Contemporary features	800	CP
10–1113	400E Steam Locomotive and Tender Crackle Black; 1999		
	(**–0**) Standard gauge with Traditional features	800	CP
	(**–1**) Standard gauge with Contemporary features	800	CP

		MSRP	Current
Electric Locomotives			
(0-4-0)			
10–1066	9E Electric Locomotive Two-tone Green; 1998		
	(**–0**) Standard gauge with Traditional features	500	495
	(**–1**) Standard gauge with Contemporary features	500	485
10–1067	9E Electric Locomotive Gray/Nickel; 1998		
	(**–0**) Standard gauge with Traditional features	496	490
	(**–1**) Standard gauge with Contemporary features	500	400

10-1066 9E (0-4-0) Electric Locomotive (Two-tone Green)
10-1067 9E (0-4-0) Electric Locomotive (Gray)

10-1022 408E (0-4-4-0) Electric Locomotive (Green)
10-1023 408E (0-4-4-0) Electric Locomotive (Two-tone Brown)

		MSRP	Current
10–1104	9E Electric Locomotive		
	Orange; 1999		
	(–0) Standard gauge with Traditional		
	features	**550**	**CP**
	(–1) Standard gauge with Contemporary		
	features	**550**	**CP**
10–1105	9E Electric Locomotive		
	Dark Green; 1999		
	(–0) Standard gauge with Traditional		
	features	**550**	**CP**
	(–1) Standard gauge with Contemporary		
	features	**550**	**CP**
(0-4-4-0)			
10–1022	408E Electric Locomotive		
	Green; 1996		
	(–) Standard gauge	**600**	**600**

		MSRP	Current
10–1023	408E Electric Locomotive		
	Two-tone Brown; 1996		
	(–) Standard gauge	**599**	**850**
(4-4-4)			
10–1077	381 Electric Locomotive		
	State Green; 1998		
	(–0) Standard gauge with Traditional		
	features	**600**	**700**
	(–1) Standard gauge with Contemporary		
	features	**600**	**700**

Rolling Stock

Boxcars, Stock Cars, and Refrigerator Cars

Boxcars

10–1109	200 Series MTH Boxcar		
	Purple/Gray; 1999	**130**	**CP**

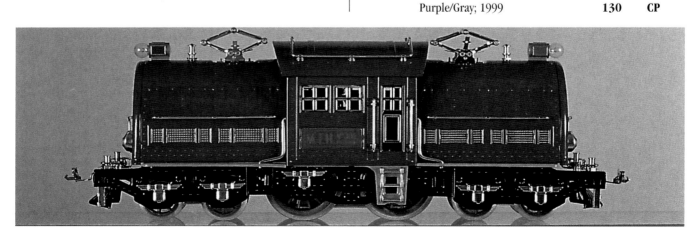

10-1077 381 (4-4-4) Electric Locomotive (State Set locomotive)

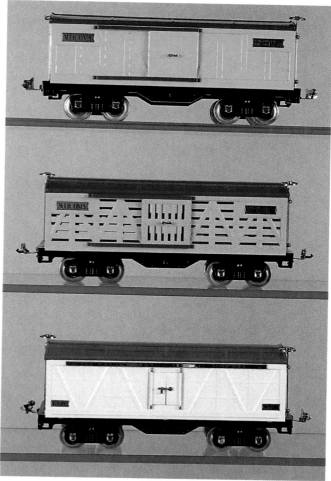

10-1085 500 Series Boxcar 514
10-1088 500 Series Cattle Car 513
10-1089 500 Series Refrigerated Car 514R

		MSRP	Current
10–1085	500 Series Boxcar numbered 514 Yellow/Brown; 1998	120	125
10–1086	500 Series Boxcar Cream; 1998	120	125
10–3003	800 Series Boxcar Orange/Brown; 1999	80	CP
Stock Cars			
10–1087	500 Series Cattle Car numbered 513 Green/Orange; 1998	120	125
10–1088	500 Series Cattle Car numbered 513 Cream/Maroon; 1998	120	125
10–3005	800 Series Cattle Car Tuscan; 1999	80	CP
Refrigerator Cars			
10–1089	500 Series Reefer Car numbered 514R White/Blue lettered "MTH Lines Ventilated Refrigerator"; 1998	120	125
10–1090	500 Series Reefer Car Ivory/Peacock; 1998	120	125
10–3008	800 Series Reefer Car White/Brown; 1999	80	CP
Cabooses			
10–1054	200 Series New York Central Caboose numbered 217 Red; 1997	130	150
10–1055	200 Series Caboose Peacock/Red; 1997	130	150

10–1109 200 Series Boxcar Black; 1999   130   CP

10-1054 200 Series New York Central Caboose 217

10-1071 200 Series Flatcar (w/wood load)
10-1073 200 Series Gondola Car (w/3 REA containers)

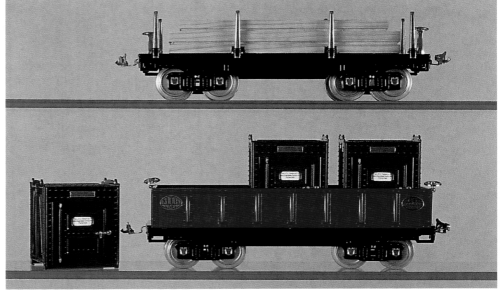

		MSRP	Current
10–1098	500 Series Caboose Nickel; 1999	**120**	**CP**
10–1099	500 Series Caboose Brass; 1999	**120**	**CP**
10–3004	800 Series Caboose Red/Brown; 1999	**90**	**CP**

Flatcars

		MSRP	Current
10–1071	200 Series Flatcar; includes wood load Black; 1998	**100**	**110**
10–1072	200 Series Flatcar Black; 1998	**100**	**110**
10–1117	500 Series Flatcar Dark Green; 1999	**90**	**CP**
10–1118	500 Series Flatcar Lt. Green; 1999	**90**	**CP**

Gondolas

		MSRP	Current
10–1073	200 Series Gondola Car numbered 21; includes three New York Central Railway Express containers Maroon; 1998	**140**	**190**
10–1074	200 Series Gondola Car Med. Green; 1998	**140**	**165**
10–1119	500 Series Gondola Car Peacock; 1999	**90**	**CP**

		MSRP	Current
10–1119	500 Series Gondola Car Black; 1999	**90**	**CP**
10–3006	800 Series Gondola Car Orange; 1999	**70**	**CP**

Hopper and Dump Cars

Hopper Cars

		MSRP	Current
10–1052	200 Series Hopper Car Green/Nickel; 1997	**130**	**150**
10–1053	200 Series Hopper Car numbered 216; includes coal load Dark Green/Brass; 1997	**130**	**150**
10–1100	500 Series Hopper Car Nickel; 1999	**120**	**CP**
10–1101	500 Series Hopper Car Brass; 1999	**120**	**CP**
10–3007	800 Series Hopper Car Black; 1999	**80**	**CP**

Dump Cars

		MSRP	Current
10–1083	200 Series Dump Car Mojave; 1998	**140**	**150**
10–1084	200 Series Dump Car numbered 218 Mojave; 1998	**140**	**150**

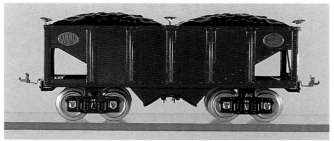

10-1053 200 Series Hopper Car (w/load) 216

10-1051 200 Series Tank Car 215

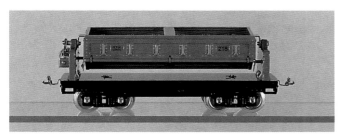

10-1084 200 Series Dump Car 218

10-1076 200 Series Searchlight Car

		MSRP	Current
Tank Cars			
10–1050	200 Series Tank Car Orange/Nickel; 1997	**130**	**150**
10–1051	200 Series Tank Car numbered 215 Green/Brass; 1997	**130**	**150**
10–1102	500 Series Tank Car Nickel; 1999	**120**	**CP**
10–1103	500 Series Tank Car Brass; 1999	**120**	**CP**

		MSRP	Current
Work Cars			
Crane Cars			
10–1081	200 Series Crane Car Yellow/Green/Red/Black; 1998	**200**	**200**
10–1082	200 Series Crane Car Peacock; 1998	**200**	**200**
Searchlight Cars			
10–1075	200 Series Searchlight Car Terra-Cotta; 1998	**140**	**150**

10-1081 200 Series Crane Car

10-1042 800 Series 4-Car Freight Set
        Gondola 812
        Boxcar 814
        Hopper 816
        Caboose 817

10-1065 4-Car 613 Series Passenger Car Set
        Baggage 615
        Pullman 612
        Pullman 613
        Observation Car 614

		MSRP	Current
10–1076	200 Series Searchlight Car Med. Green; 1998	140	150
10–1115	500 Series Searchlight Car Black/Terra-Cotta; 1999	130	CP
10–1116	500 Series Searchlight Car Black/Green; 1999	130	CP

Mixed Sets

		MSRP	Current
10–1042	800 Series 4-Car Freight Set; Various; 1996	250	260

		MSRP	Current

Passenger Cars

		MSRP	Current
10–1024	4-Car 613 Series Passenger Car Set Green; 1996	399	450
10–1025	4-Car 613 Series Passenger Car Set Terra-Cotta; 1996	399	450
10–1064	4-Car 613 Series Passenger Car Set Blue; 1998	400	450
10–1065	4-Car 613 Series Passenger Car Set Red/Silver; 1998	400	425

10-1068 4-Car Stephen Girard Passenger Car Set
Coach "Liberty Bell" 424
Coach "Stephen Girard" 425
Coach "Philadelphia" 427
Observation Car "Coral Isle" 426

10-1078 4-Car State Passenger Car Set
Coach "California" 412
Coach "Colorado" 413
(10-1079 Coach "Illinois" 414 separate sale only)
Solarium "Maryland" 415
Observation Car "New York" 416

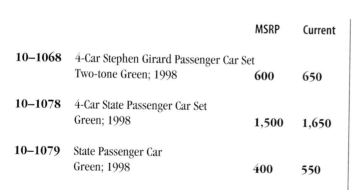

		MSRP	Current
10–1068	4-Car Stephen Girard Passenger Car Set Two-tone Green; 1998	**600**	**650**
10–1078	4-Car State Passenger Car Set Green; 1998	**1,500**	**1,650**
10–1079	State Passenger Car Green; 1998	**400**	**550**

		MSRP	Current
10–1106	4-Car 418 Series Passenger Car Set Orange; 1999	**600**	**CP**
10–1107	4-Car 418 Series Passenger Car Set Dark Green; 1999	**600**	**CP**
10–1114	4-Car *Blue Comet* Passenger Car Set Blue; 1999	**1,200**	**CP**

RailKing, Premier, and Tinplate Traditions Line Accessories

O Gauge Accessories

Signs, Signals, and Lights

		MSRP
30-1019	No. 54 Street Lamp Set; Maroon; 1996	25
30-1020	No. 54 Street Lamp Set; Green; 1996	25
30-1026	No. 56 Gas Lamp Set; Green; 1996	25
30-1027	No. 56 Gas Lamp Set; Maroon; 1996	25
30-1028	No. 57 Corner Lamp Set; Yellow; 1996	25
30-1029	No. 57 Corner Lamp Set; Orange; 1996	25
30-1030	No. 59 Gooseneck Lamp Set; Maroon; 1996	25
30-1031	No. 59 Gooseneck Lamp Set; Green; 1996	25
30-1032	No. 64 Highway Lamp Set; Green; 1996	20
30-1033	No. 64 Highway Lamp Set; Maroon; 1996	20
30-1034*	No. 153 Operating Block Signal; Green; 1996 *CTT 7/97	30
30-1035A*	No. 151 Operating Semaphore; Black; 1996 *CTT 7/97	30
30-1036	No. 69 Operating Warning Bell; Maroon; 1996	30
30-1057	No. 58 Lamp Set, Single Arc; Pea Green; 1997	25
30-1058	No. 35 Street Lamp Set; Gray; 1997	25
30-1059	No. 35 Street Lamp Set; Aluminum; 1997	25
30-1060	No. 70 Yard Lamp Set; Black; 1997	20
30-1062	O Scale Set, Hexagonal; Black; 1997	20
30-1065	No. 64 Highway Lamp Set; Dark Green; 1997	20
30-1066	No. 54 Double Arc Lamp Set; Dark Brown; 1997	28
30-1067	No. 59 Gooseneck Lamp Set; Cream; 1997	25
30-1068	No. 57 Corner Lamp Set; Gray; 1997	25
30-1069	No. 56 Gas Lamp Set; Bronze; 1997	25
30-1070	No. 580-1 Teardrop Lamp Set; Green; 1997	20
30-1071	No. 580-2 Teardrop Lamp Set; Green; 1997	20
30-1073	No. 262 Crossing Gate/Signal; Black; 1997	40
30-1074	No. 154 Highway Flashing Signal; Black; 1997	30
30-1075	No. 151 Operating Semaphore; Green; 1997	30
30-1076	No. 153 Operating Block Signal; Black; 1997	30
30-1077	No. 69 Operating Warning Bell; Maroon; 1997	30
30-1078	O Scale Lamp Set, Round; Black; 1997	20
30-1078A	No. 580-1 Teardrop Lamp Set; Silver; 1997	20
30-1079	O Scale Lamp Set, Square; Black; 1997	20
30-1079A	No. 580-1 Teardrop Lamp Set; Pea Green; 1997	20
30-1080	No. 47 Crossing Gate and Signal; Green; 1997	80
30-1080A	No. 580-2 Teardrop Lamp Set; Pea Green; 1997	20
30-1081A	No. 580-2 Teardrop Lamp Set; Maroon; 1997	20
30-1082A	No. 580-2 Teardrop Lamp Set; Silver; 1997	20
30-1089-1	Traffic Light Set, Single Lamp; Silver/Yellow; 1998	20
30-1089-2	Traffic Light Set, Double Lamp; Silver/Yellow; 1998	25
30-1090	No. 58 Lamp Set, Single Arc; Maroon; 1998	25
30-1093	Operating Banjo Signal; Black; 1998	30
30-1095	No. 64 Highway Lamp Set; Silver; 1998	20
30-1096	No. 54 Street Lamp Set; Cream; 1998	28
30-1097	No. 57 Corner Lamp Set; Cream; 1998	25
30-1098	No. 56 Gas Lamp Set; Black; 1998	28
30-1099	No. 35 Street Lamp Set; Pea Green; 1998	25
30-9025	No. 395 Floodlight Tower; Yellow; 1999	40
30-9026	No. 450 Signal Bridge; Black; 1999	45
30-11001	No. 35 Street Lamp Set; Red; 1998	25
30-11002	No. 58 Lamp Set, Single Arc; Dark Green; 1998	25
30-11003	No. 64 Highway Lamp Set; Black; 1998	20
30-11005	O Scale Operating Block Signal; Silver; 1998	30
30-11006	O Scale Modern Operating Crossing Signal; Silver; 1998	50
30-11008	No. 152 Operating Crossing Gate; Red/Aluminum; 1999	30
30-11009	O Scale Cantilevered Signal Bridge; Silver; 1999	50
30-11010	O Scale Operating Crossing Signal; Black; 1999	60
30-11011	O Scale Dwarf Signal; Black; 1999	25
30-11012	O Scale Operating Crossing Gate Signal; Silver; 1999	60
30-11013	O Scale 7-Light Block Signal; Black; 1999	35
30-11014	O Scale Operating Crossing Flasher w/sound; Silver; 1999	50

Structures

30-1031	Operating Street Clock; Green; 1998	25
30-1056	High-Tension Tower Set; Silver; 1997	60
30-1061	Operating Street Clock; Red; 1997	25
30-1072	Operating Street Clock; Teal; 1997	25
30-1086	Sinclair Die-Cast Fuel Truck; N/A; 1998	13

30-1087	Road Sign Set; Brown/White; 1998	13
30-1088	Telephone Pole Set; Brown; 1998	15
30-1094	Operating Street Clock; Dark Green; 1998	30
30-9001	No. 6 Farm House; Gray/Yellow; 1996	30
30-9002	No. 5 Country Church; White/Gray; 1996	30
30-9003	No. 4 Country House; White/Red/Gray; 1997	28
30-9004	Hobby Shop; Red/Gray; 1997	40
30-9005	Passenger Station w/dual platforms; Orange; 1997	80
30-9006	Passenger Station Platform; Black/Gray; 1997	20
30-9007	No. 6 Farm House; Yellow; 1997	30
30-9008	No. 4 Country House; Blue; 1997	30
30-9010	Sinclair Oil Refinery; White/Green; 1998	150
30-9011	Switch Tower; Gray/Blue; 1998	30
30-9012	Corner Drug Store; Red/Gray; 1998	30
30-9013	4-Story Building; Gray; 1998	40
30-9014	Passenger Station w/dual platforms; Red; 1998	80
30-9015	No. 4 Country House; Tan; 1999	30
30-9016	No. 6 Farm House; Maroon; 1999	30
30-9017	Corner Bank; Gray; 1999	40
30-9018	Hardware Store; Red/Gray; 1999	40
30-9022	No. 334 Dispatch Board; Tan; 1999	100
30-9023	Row House no. 1; Beige; 1999	25
30-9024	Row House no. 2; Gray; 1999	25
30-9027	No. 455 Oil Derrick; Red/Green; 1999	80
30-9028	Oil Pumping Station; Green/Blue; 1999	50
30-9029	No. 193 Industrial Water Tower; Gray/Black; 1999	50
30-9101*	Sinclair Operating Gas Station; White/Green; 1997 *CTT 5/98	100
30-9102	Operating Firehouse; Red; 1997	130
30-9103	Operating Flag; Red; 1997	30
30-9104	Operating Car Wash; White; 1998	130
30-9105	Operating Drive-in Diner; Green; 1998	130
30-9106	Esso Operating Gas Station; Red/White; 1998	130
30-9107	Operating Passenger Station w/people; Silver/Brown; 1998	N/A
30-9109	Union 76 Operating Gas Station; White/Orange; 1999	130
30-11007	O Scale Water Column; Black; 1999	20
30-50002	Fence Set; White; 1998	15
30-50004	Big Mo Die-Cast Trailer; Orange; 1999	25

Bridges and Tunnels

30-6135	O Scale Steel Arch Bridge; Silver; 1999	60
30-9020	O Scale Hell Gate Bridge; Red/Gray; 1999	200
30-9021	O Scale Hell Gate Bridge; Cream/Green; 1999	200
40-1013	O Scale Steel Arch Bridge; Maroon; 1998	60
40-1014	O Scale Bridge Girder; Silver; 1998	20
40-1032	O Scale Bridge Girder; Maroon; 1999	20
40-9014	Tunnel Portal, Single; Tan; 1998	15
40-9015	Tunnel Portal, Double; Tan; 1998	20

Track and Switches

40-1001	RealTrax 10″ Straight; Gray; 1998	4
40-1001-4	RealTrax 10″ Straight Hanger (4 pcs.); Gray; 1999	15
40-1002	RealTrax O31 Curve; Gray; 1997	4
40-1002-4	RealTrax O31 Curve Hanger (4 pcs.); Gray; 1999	15
40-1003	RealTrax Lighted Lockon; Gray; 1998	5
40-1004	RealTrax O31 Switch (R); Gray; 1998	50
40-1005	RealTrax O31 Switch (L); Gray; 1998	50
40-1006	RealTrax 90° Crossover; Gray; 1998	20
40-1007	RealTrax 45° Crossover; Gray; 1999	20
40-1008	RealTrax Uncoupling Section; Gray; 1998	30
40-1010	RealTrax O72 Curve; Gray; 1998	5
40-1011	RealTrax Adapter Straight; Gray; 1998	8
40-1012	RealTrax 5.5″ Straight; Gray; 1998	8
40-1012-2	RealTrax 5.5″ Straight Hanger (2 pcs.); Gray; 1998	8
40-1015	RealTrax Wire Harness; Red/Black; 1998	4
40-1016	RealTrax 5.0″ Straight; Red/Black; 1998	4
40-1016-2	RealTrax 5.0″ Straight Hanger (2 pcs.); Red/Black; 1998	4
40-1017	RealTrax 4.25″ Straight; Red/Black; 1998	4
40-1017-2	RealTrax 4.25″ Straight Hanger (2 pcs.); Red/Black; 1998	4
40-1018	RealTrax 3.5″ Straight; Red/Black; 1998	4
40-1018-2	RealTrax 3.5″ Straight Hanger (2 pcs.); Red/Black; 1998	4
40-1019	RealTrax 30″ Straight; Red/Black; 1998	4
40-1020	RealTrax O72 Switch (R); Gray; 1998	70
40-1021	RealTrax O72 Switch (L); Gray; 1998	70

40-1022	RealTrax O31 Half Curve; Gray; 1998	4
40-1022-2	RealTrax O31 Half Curve; Blister-Carded; Gray; 1998	8
40-1023	Layout Builder (8 pcs.); Gray; 1999	30
40-1024	RealTrax Bumper; Gray; 1999	13
40-1025	RealTrax Figure 8 Layout Builder; Gray; 1999	50
40-1026	RealTrax Left Track Siding Layout Builder; Gray; 1999	80
40-1027	RealTrax Right Track Siding Layout Builder; Gray; 1999	80
40-1028	RealTrax Track Activation Device (ITAD); Gray; 1999	20
40-1029	RealTrax 10″ Insulated Straight; Gray; 1999	20
40-1037	O Gauge Track Activation Device; Black; 1996	10
40-1042	RealTrax O42 Curve; Gray; 1999	4
40-1043	RealTrax O42 Switch (R); Gray; 1999	50
40-1044	RealTrax O42 Switch (L); Gray; 1999	50
40-1045-2	RealTrax O42 Half Curve Track; Carded; Gray; 1999	8
40-9901	RealTrax Layout Design no. 1; Gray; 1999	400
40-9902	RealTrax Layout Design no. 2; Gray; 1999	480
40-9903	RealTrax Layout Design no. 3; Gray; 1999	420
40-9904	RealTrax Layout Design no. 4; Gray; 1999	571
40-9905	RealTrax Layout Design no. 5; Gray; 1999	330
40-9906	RealTrax Layout Design no. 6; Gray; 1999	350
40-9907	RealTrax Layout Design no. 7; Gray; 1999	560
40-9908	RealTrax Layout Design no. 8; Gray; 1999	420
40-9909	RealTrax Layout Design no. 9; Gray; 1999	620
40-9910	RealTrax Layout Design no. 10; Gray; 1999	500
40-9911	RealTrax Layout Design no. 11; Gray; 1999	730
40-9912	RealTrax Layout Design no. 12; Gray; 1999	490
40-9913	RealTrax Layout Design no. 13; Gray; 1999	490
40-9914	RealTrax Layout Design no. 14; Gray; 1999	830
45-1001	ScaleTrax 10″ Straight; Gray; 1999	830
45-1002	ScaleTrax O31 Curve; Brown; 1999	4
45-1002-4	ScaleTrax O31 Curve Hanger (4 pcs.); Brown; 1999	15
45-1003	ScaleTrax O31 Switch (LH); Brown; 1999	50
45-1004	ScaleTrax O31 Switch (RH); Brown; 1999	50
45-1005	ScaleTrax 90° Crossover Track; Brown; 1999	20
45-1006	ScaleTrax 45° Crossover Track; Brown; 1999	20
45-1007	ScaleTrax O54 Curve; Brown; 1999	4
45-1007-4	ScaleTrax O54 Curve Hanger (4 pcs.); Brown; 1999	15
45-1008	ScaleTrax O54 Switch (LH); Brown; 1999	50
45-1009	ScaleTrax O54 Switch (RH); Brown; 1999	50
45-1010	ScaleTrax O72 Curve; Brown; 1999	5
45-1011	ScaleTrax 3.5″ Straight; Brown; 1999	5
45-1011-2	ScaleTrax 3.5″ Straight Hanger (2 pcs.); Brown; 1999	5
45-1012	ScaleTrax 4.25″ Straight; Brown; 1999	5
45-1012-2	ScaleTrax 4.25″ Straight Hanger (2 pcs.); Brown; 1999	5
45-1013	ScaleTrax 5.0″ Straight; Brown; 1999	5
45-1013-2	ScaleTrax 5.0″ Straight Hanger (2 pcs.); Brown; 1999	5
45-1014	ScaleTrax 5.5″ Straight; Brown; 1999	5
45-1014-2	ScaleTrax 5.5″ Straight Hanger (2 pcs.); Brown; 1999	5
45-1015	ScaleTrax 22° Crossover Track; Brown; 1999	20
45-1019	ScaleTrax 30″ Straight; Brown; 1999	20
45-1020	ScaleTrax O72 Switch (R); Brown; 1999	50
45-1021	ScaleTrax O72 Switch (L); Brown; 1999	50

Transformers

20-Z2000	Transformer; Black; 1995	NM
40-750	Z-750 Transformer; Black; 1998	80
40-4000*	Z-4000 Transformer; Black; 1998 *CTT 9/98	399
40-4001	Z-4000 Remote Commander System; Black; 1999	80
40-4002	Z-4000 Remote Commander Receiver; Black; 1999	40

Standard Gauge Accessories

Signs, Signals, and Lights

10-1044	No. 92 Floodlight Tower Set; Terra Cotta/Green; 1996	130
10-1046	No. 79 Operating Crossing Signal; Cream; 1997	50
10-1047	No. 80 Operating Semaphore; Orange; 1997	50
10-1048	No. 99 Operating Block Signal; Red; 1997	50
10-1049	No. 438 Tinplate Signal Tower; Red/White; 1997	100
10-1096	No. 87 Railroad Crossing Signal; Dark Green/White; 1999	40
10-1097	No. 78 Standard Gauge Block Signal; Orange/Cream; 1999	60

Structures

10-200	No. 200 Turntable; Green; 1999	200
10-1043	No. 94 High-Tension Tower Set; Red/Silver; 1996	130
10-1057	No. 155 Freight Shed; Red/Tan; 1997	250
10-1069	No. 441 Weigh Scale; Green/Beige; 1998	300
10-1070	No. 116 Passenger Station; White/Red; 1998	300

10-1093	No. 71 Telegraph Post Set; Gray/Red; 1999	50
10-1094	No. 71 Telegraph Post Set; Peacock/Red; 1999	50
10-1095	No. 67 Lamp Post Set; Dark Green; 1999	40
10-1108	No. 63 Lamp Post Set; Aluminum; 1999	40
10-1110	No. 192 Villa Set; Various; 1999	200
10-1111	No. 444 Roundhouse Section; Orange; 1999	500
10-1121	No. 437 Switch Tower; Tan/Brown; 1999	250

Bridges

10-1015	Hell Gate Bridge; Cream/Green; 1994	499
10-1016	Hell Gate Bridge; White/Silver/Red; 1994	499

Track and Switches

10-1021	Lighted Lockon; Black; 1996	4
10-1037	Standard Gauge Track Activation Device; Silver; 1996	10
10-1038	Standard Gauge Straight; Silver; 1996	4
10-1039	Standard Gauge Curved; Silver; 1998	4
10-1040	Standard Gauge Straight, Wide Radius; Silver; 1996	4
10-1041	Standard Gauge Curve, Wide Radius; Silver; 1996	4
10-4001	Standard Gauge Switch (RH); Green; 1999	80
10-4002	Standard Gauge Switch (LH); Green; 1999	80
10-4003	Standard Gauge Switch (RH), Wide Radius; Green; 1999	90
10-4004	Standard Gauge Switch (LH), Wide Radius; Green; 1999	90

Transformers

10-1017	Powerhouse; Cream/Orange; 1995	549
10-1018	Powerhouse; White/Red; 1995	549
10-1080	No. 436 Powerhouse; Terra Cotta; 1998	130

Toys

10-1001	Hi-Way Henry Operating Tin Toy; N/A; 1993	300
10-1002	Amos & Andy Operating Tin Toy; N/A; 1993	300
10-1003	Kingsbury Fire House & Pumper; N/A; 1993	495
10-1004	Robby Space Patrol Operating Robot; N/A; 1993	500
10-1010	Mr. Atomic Tinplate Toy; Silver; 1993	500
10-1011	Show Case Mr. Atomic; N/A; 19N/A	80
10-1014	Mr. Atomic Tinplate Toy; Blue; 1993	500

Miscellaneous Replacement Accessories and Promotional Products

Miscellaneous Replacement Accessories

20-30001	MTH Junk Load; Gray; 1998	10
20-30002	MTH Coal Load; Black; 1998	5
30-50001	MTH Coal Load; Gray; 1998	5
30-50003	MTH Junk Load; Black; 1998	7
30-50005	Bag of Coal; White; 1999	3
60-1045	ProtoSmoke Fluid 7oz.; White; 1997	10
60-1063	ProtoSmoke Fluid; N/A; 1997	100
60-1064	25-piece Case 1-oz. Smoke Fluid; N/A; 1997	100

Promotional Products

60-1320	MTH Video, History; N/A; 1999	10
60-1321	MTH Book, History; N/A; 1999	30
60-1322	RealTrax Track Layout Software; N/A; 1999	80
AA-1993	Consumer Catalog, "Fall 1993"; Dash 8s; 1993	N/A
AB-1994	Consumer Catalog, "Spring 1994"; UP Challenger; 1994	N/A
AC-1994	Consumer Catalog, "Fall 1994"; Southern Ps-4; 1994	N/A
AD-1994	Consumer Catalog, "Winter 1994"; F3s; 1994	N/A
AE-1995	Consumer Catalog, "15th Anniversary"; N&W Y6b; 1995	N/A
AF-1995	Consumer Catalog, "Fall 1995"; Santa Fe 4-8-4; 1995	N/A
AG-1995	Consumer Catalog, "Winter 1995"; NYC Empire State; 1995	N/A
AH-1996	Consumer Catalog, "Spring 1996"; C&O Allegheny; 1996	N/A
AI-1996	Consumer Catalog, "Summer 1996"; PRR K-4s; 1996	N/A
AJ-1996	Consumer Catalog, "Fall/Winter 1996"; NYC J-1e; 1996	N/A
AK-1997	Consumer Catalog, "Spring 1997"; UP Big Boy; 1997	N/A
AL-1997	Consumer Catalog, "1997 Volume 1"; WVPP Shay; 1997	N/A
AM-1997	Consumer Catalog, "1997 Volume 2"; N&W J; 1997	N/A
AN-1998	Consumer Catalog, "1998 Volume 1"; BNSF Dash 9; 1997	N/A
AO-1998	Consumer Catalog, "1998 Volume 2"; Blue Comet; 1998	N/A
AP-1998	Consumer Catalog, "1998 Volume 3"; SP Daylight; 1998	N/A
AQ-1999	Consumer Catalog, "1999 Volume 1"; Camelback; 1999	N/A
AR-1999	Consumer Catalog, "1999 Volume 2"; Berkshire; 1999	N/A
AS-1999	Consumer Catalog, "1999 Volume 3"; F59PH; 1999	N/A

Note: Only MSRP is given for this section, as very few items have shown a notable appreciation in value, the most notable exception being 30-9101 ($180).

Index

Index